Missing Person

Missing Person

Karen A. Metcalfe

BOOCHIE
PUBLISHING

For information regarding permission, write to:
Boochie Publishing
Post Office Box 200092
Arlington, TX 76006
www.boochiepublishing.com

Disclaimer: This story is about the author's personal experiences and should be used for informational purposes only and does not provide an official diagnosis. Used for its intended purpose; this book can promote mental health awareness. Consult with your doctor or a licensed professional for more information, diagnosis, and treatment options. Additionally, if you or someone you know is struggling with a mental health problem, you should seek the services of a physician or appropriate licensed professional as soon as possible. If you feel like you have a life-threatening emergency, if you're having thoughts of suicide or hurting someone else, please call 911, contact your local emergency authorities or go to a hospital immediately.

Bible verses are quoted from the King James Version of the Holy Bible unless noted otherwise. Any reference to satan is lowercase intentionally.

References and Resources:
The National Institute of Mental Health | www.nimh.nih.gov | Accessed August 2019
Laura A. Pratt, Ph.D., and Debra J. Brody, M.P.H.| Centers for Disease Control and Prevention | www.cdc.gov | Depression in the U.S. household population, 2009–2012. NCHS data brief, no 172. Hyattsville, MD: National Center for Health Statistics. December 2014 | Accessed August 2019
Mayo Clinic | Mayo Foundation for Medical Education and Research www.mayoclinic.org | Accessed August 2019
Jason Silverstein | CBS News | Mass Shootings 2019 | www.cbsnews.com | August 5, 2019 | Accessed August 2019
That's Enough Lyrics – Angela Spivey | www.elyrics.net/read/a/angela-spivey-lyrics/that_s-enough-lyrics.html | Accessed September 2019
www.biblegateway.com | Accessed September 2019
Anxiety and Depression Association of America| https://adaa.org/understanding-anxiety/related-illnesses/eating-disorders | Eating Disorders | Accessed August 2019
Dr. Kristie Leong | Foods That Can Cause Panic Attacks - Health Guide Info. www.healthguideinfo.com/panic-disorder | Accessed August 2019
www.washingtonpost.com | Accessed July 2019
National Alliance of Mental Health | www.nami.org
National Suicide Prevention Lifeline | suicidepreventionlifeline.org | 1-800-273-8255

In Loving Memory of

Peggy Ann Reynolds

May 1949 – August 2007

My Dear Sister,

Life has not been the same without you!

I love and miss you so much,

Your Boochie Baby

Table of Contents

DEDICATION

This book is dedicated to my mother and my children.

Mom, thanks for introducing me to Jesus Christ at an early age. You consistently lived a life of holiness and will always be my greatest example of true salvation. You are continually reminding me that I am different and unique, but as long as I have Jesus, I will be fine. I cherish the words of wisdom that you share during our daily talks. Your unconditional love is matchless.

I love you very much!

***

Lauren and LeRoy, thank you for being my chauffeurs, nurses, and for the countless hours that you spent with me in the hospital, never complaining. I am forever grateful for the sacrifices that you made and your love and support throughout this journey.

Mommy loves you the most!

Special Thanks

Special thanks to my siblings for all you do to show that I am your favorite.

I love each of you more than words can express.

***

Thank you to all the women who have stayed and prayed with me through thick and thin; never giving up on me. I do not know many people who can say they have the support of so many phenomenal women.

***

TESTIMONIALS

Thank you for working so hard for us! I know you have been through a lot and writing can sometimes have you relive what you have been through, but without your story, none of what we do would be possible.

Thank you for being you, one hundred percent of the time no matter what people have told you, done to you and even the way they treated you. That is what makes you special. I am glad the journey you are on now will allow you not to become a MISSING PERSON again. You currently have a new stage and light to tell your story.

You deserve all the attention. You are made for this. I am glad to be a part of your story.

Love,
Leroy W. Anderson II

TESTIMONIALS

Karen is an author in her own right. She tells her story about panic attacks and other issues that will help you, your family and friends who may be dealing with these issues.

Holloway Gray
Author of Walking in The Shadow of Greatness

***

Karen's love for people has always been validated by her acts of kindness and her willingness to help them be better. Her million-dollar smile radiates a message of freedom and joy.

Paula Hearn

FORWARD

From the time I met Karen in an interview for the position of Executive Assistant, I have felt that she could do anything. Today, I totally feel the same way. Our relationship has developed over the years and we have always respected one another professionally. If I were to list all of the incredible accomplishments Karen has achieved for others, the list would be very long. She has earned the respect of everyone she has supported, based on her incredible project management talents and amazing desire to help others.

To my surprise, after knowing her for more than twenty years, Karen has decided to unveil her life-long secret, her struggle with panic attacks, as a way to bring awareness to this disability, share her story as a way to tell your story, and begin to remove the stigma associated with mental illness. While we all face some form of stereotype, individuals with disabilities are no exception.

In nine months, I have seen Karen struggle with putting herself first, caring about what others would say if they knew she had a mental illness, and being told that she would struggle with getting a job. This is Karen's mission. God prepares us for what is ahead of us. Her struggle with hiding her disability is now being used to lead others out of the shadows of fear, embarrassment, or being defined by their mental illness.

Missing Person, written simply, clearly, and practically, based on Karen's experiences will challenge your assumptions, biases, and stereotypes about people with mental illness. Used as it is intended, this book serves as a guide to help those you know and meet realize that mental illness does not mean incapable of being successful.

Coach Liz Moffitt
Certified Master Coach

DEAR JOHN,

When we first met, you took my breath away! You whispered things in my ear that caused my heart to flutter, my pulse to race, and my knees to weaken.

Sometimes you started with a subtle undertone in my ear. I ignored you, so you spoke louder until you captured my undivided attention. Other times, you surprised me and knocked me off my feet for minutes, hours, and sometimes days.

I thought our relationship was unique. I was ashamed to let anyone know about us because you caused me so much pain and grief!

I recently heard that you treat others the same way you were treating me. You knew that if I told others about us, I could have avoided your shenanigans, and our relationship would have become nonexistent years ago.

Well, enough, is enough! Your secret is out!

Now that I have been researching, reflecting, and

discussing us, I found out that you are nothing but a
HABITUAL LIAR!

I am writing to tell you that we can no longer spend
time together. I never want to see you again!

I had weapons that I should have used to keep you
away, but you pulled the wool over my eyes, I thought
that you left for good, so I did not use them.

Here you come, years later, sneaking back in when I
was not paying attention, especially during significant life
events. You knew that I was vulnerable, so you used
these trying times as an opportunity to display your
craftiness. Your drama caused me nervousness, misery,
and despair.

You showed up in my life quietly and caused me to
alienate myself from others. Your presence forced me to
act in ways that I never imagined.

Lately, your visits have become more frequent,
intense, and more abusive. You knew what you were

doing, that you were not welcome, and that I had bolted the doors to my heart. But I did not realize that it was not my heart that you were after.

You wanted to control my mind.

You forced your way in over and over again, by using different tactics.

You started causing me to experience things that did not make sense; things that caused society to use the "C" word to describe our relationship.

One day when my arms were aching, you wanted me to think that I was having a heart attack. What about the time when my thumb was cramped, and you wanted me to believe that I was having a stroke?

Not to mention the time years ago when you tried to make me think that I had a brain tumor. As I look back, one of the puzzling things about this is that I was so wrapped up into what you were saying that I did not notice that my head was not hurting.

Dear John

You make me sick to my stomach!

You have caused me to lose weight, not eat, and worry about every little thing.

You have cost me time, money, and relationships. You tried to take my life.

For years, you have been telling me that I was going to die. You say those things to keep me from living. I will die someday, but not today.

You like to prey on kind-hearted people, especially — those who do not like confrontation and confusion.

I especially hate it when you wait until I am alone to visit. You managed to creep into my sleep a few times, which pissed me off the most.

Did a Christian say, PISSED? You often tried to make me think that I was not a Christian because I was spending time with you.

DEAR JOHN

You are nothing but a bully and what the Bible calls a roaring lion, seeking whom you may devour.

You also look for people with certain medical conditions and people who are taking certain medications. You pick on them when they are weak. But once they recover from their sickness, they kick you out; put you in your rightful place and never have to see you again.

Eventually, you will learn that the more you bother me, the more people I will tell about you and your wicked ways. I have posted your picture everywhere possible, so don't try to get away this time. Once others find out about you, they will join me in reporting you. We will have a solid case to destroy you once and for all.

Oh, I have one more thing to say. I am throwing out all of your belongings: including doubt, pain, insecurity, low self-esteem, depression, and fear. These things belong to you, and they must leave with you so that you will not have a reason to return.

After years of trying to get rid of you on my own, I now

have the support and resources necessary to force you to leave me alone once and for all.

It's past time for you to leave.

From this day forward, I will ignore you like you have ignored my commands to leave.

Previously yours,

Panic Attack Conqueror

ABOUT THE BOOK

Have you ever found yourself suddenly gasping for air for no apparent reason? Did this feeling cause you to be afraid that something terrible was about to happen? Then your heart started beating so fast, hard, and loud that you thought that you were about to die? Once the symptoms subsided, were you exhausted and afraid that it would occur again?

The first time this happened to me, it cost me over six-hundred dollars in medical bills. Why? Because I could not explain what this irregular feeling was or why it came over me. So, I caught a taxi to the emergency room and discovered that I had a panic attack.

In this book we will take a journey that began in the late 1990s. Society forced me to believe that people who had panic attacks were crazy or could not control their emotions. It ended in 2019 where the stigma remains.

This book was written to clarify misconceptions, encourage people to get help, share ways to help you manage panic attacks, and reveal things that cause people to be ashamed to talk about mental health.

Join me for the rest of the story.

PREFACE

Mental **health** affects all of us; however, everyone does not have a mental **illness**. Many people face anxiety, depression, or sadness at some point in life. But for the person who has a mental disorder, the symptoms may linger or worsen if not treated. Some illnesses have misconceptions. For example, I once thought that obesity was the cause of diabetes and that diabetes caused all renal failure. I discovered that there are various causes of diabetes and renal failure. The same is valid for mental illness. An underlying disease, lifestyle choices, and genetics are known causes for mental illness.

Here are some essential questions to consider when discussing mental illnesses. Do we treat mental illness differently than other diseases because we do not understand it? Does mental illness play a role in mass shootings, suicide, and crime? If we knew more about mental illness, could we find ways to prevent these devastating events?

From helping our loved ones have a better quality of life to preventing mass shootings and suicides, we may all benefit from being educated about mental illness.

Mass shootings are on the rise. According to the Washington Post, between 1997-2017, there were approximately one hundred and sixty-three shootings in which a lone shooter killed four or more people. The amount of mass shootings across the U.S. so far in 2019 has outpaced the number of days this year, according to a gun violence research group. This puts 2019 on pace to be the first year since 2016 with an average of more than one mass shooting a day. After a mass shooting, we often hear that no one was aware of the shooter's mental illness. In other cases, people didn't know what to do to help the individual with the mental condition.

In 2017, suicide was the tenth leading cause of death in the United States, claiming the lives of over 47,000 people. According to the Centers of Disease Control and Prevention (CDC) WISQARS Leading Cause of Death Reporting. Cited: www.nimh.nih.gov. April 16, 2019

During 2009–2012, 7.6% of Americans aged 12 and over had depression. Depression was more prevalent among females than males and among adults aged 40–59 than those of other age groups. Cited: www.cdc.gov.

An estimated 4.7% of U.S. adults experience panic disorder at some time in their lives. But not everyone who experiences panic attacks will develop panic disorder. *Panic attacks may not be life-threatening, but they are very frightening and may alter your lifestyle.* A person who suffers from panic attacks may feel afraid that he or she is about to die. Also, they may not know why their heart is beating like it is trying to jump out of their chest. They are aware that something is not right, so they become afraid which makes the panic attack worse.

After I had a panic attack, I was exhausted and depressed, mainly because I was afraid of having another one. Here is one stigma we can eliminate about depression - everyone who experiences depression is not suicidal or homicidal.

There are many different types of mental illnesses. I am most familiar with panic attacks and non-suicidal depression. However, I do believe that all mental disorders have something in common, MISCONCEPTIONS!

Society has the misunderstanding that most people who

have a mental illness are crazy. One dictionary definition for a crazy person is someone who has reckless behavior. Let's eliminate another **misconception** today. During my panic attacks, I did not want to bother anyone or anything. I wanted to close my eyes, turn off everything, and sleep until my heart returned to a resting heart rate of under one hundred beats a minute. What is crazy about that behavior? Nothing! I have discovered that my sudden rapid heartbeat could stem as a result of several things. Some of them you will read about as I tell my story.

Missing Person lets you into the mind of a person who has suffered from panic attacks and depression for years. My vision is to promote awareness so that the subject is no longer taboo in our homes, churches, and communities.

When I first started to tell my story, I was very depressed and had panic attacks daily. Someone recently asked, *"How long did it take for you to write your book?"* My response…over twenty years.

PREFACE

Society teaches us what to do if someone has a heart attack or stroke. Yet, we avoid discussions around mental illness. What would happen if we knew the signs and knew what to do? I believe if we promote awareness and accept the condition, only then we can take action to break the stigma associated with mental illness.

You are about to embark on a journey of a young woman who managed to hide her mental illness. She worked in executive offices; was a single parent; and a Christian, but for over two decades, she managed to mask it from her closest friends and family. She has conquered her panic attacks and now uses it as a platform to help others. She is me.

While traveling through the life and mind of someone who suffered from depression; you will hear ways to support people who encounter panic attacks in your presence. I share things that I did and did not do to help me cope with panic attacks and depression.

Read as I share my story about how the depression caused my panic attacks, and panic attacks caused my depression. You will also read about how I traveled numerous times to the hospital for a rapid heartbeat. More times than I could remember because I was not counting since I expected each trip to be my last. It wasn't until my children left home that I realized; a panic attack is something that no one should experience alone.

As you continue to read, you will discover ways to identify your triggers, information about filing for disability, reasons why Christians suffer in silence, and more.

Let's remove the mask together and break the stigma associated with panic attacks. It is time for me to say, *"Things I Could Not Say Out Loud!"*

1

I CAN'T BREATHE

It was an ordinary day at the office. Phones ringing, you could hear someone striking the keys of a typewriter, the humming sound of an ancient copy machine and people talking and laughing throughout the office.

Most days, the view was beautiful from the forty-ninth floor of a seventy-two-story building. Well, that is if you like looking at mature trees, people walking or jogging to cross the street or catch the bus. You could see twenty miles in the distance on a bright sunny day. Occasionally the clouds surrounded the building and reminded me of flying in an airplane on a foggy day. There was also an airport nearby, so it was common for an airplane to soar by the glass windows. Looking at the planes was like watching a movie through 3D glasses. I often wondered if a plane was going to hit the building.

As I inhaled, my entire body stretched to open my airways, but nothing passed through. It was like the air would enter my body then stop as though it changed its mind. Did I forget how to breathe? I decided to go to the restroom to check the mirror to see if any physical changes could help me understand the irregular breathing pattern. But first, I called one of my sisters hoping to explain to her what was going on with me. But when I dialed her number, the phone rang several times before going to voicemail. I logged out of my computer and used all of my strength to push open the large glass doors that separated my desk from the lobby. As I entered the hall, I heard someone calling my name.

"Karen, you have a call. Would you like me to take a message or would you like to take the call here?" It was Hana, the

receptionist. Remembering that I just called my sister, I slowly walked towards Hana's desk.

"Who is it?"

"It's your sister. She said that she is returning your call."

"May. I. Take. The. Call. Here?"

She slowly passed me the phone receiver while she untangled the long coiled black cord.

As I was talking to my sister, the receptionist was sitting at her desk. I tried to whisper so that she would not hear me gasping for breath between words and chopping up my sentences.

"Hey. Sis!" I began speaking, but I was still unable to breathe correctly.

"Why. Am. I. Breathing. Like. This?"

"You are having a panic attack."

"What. Is. That?"

"That is why you are breathing that way."

"Breathing. What. Way?" I questioned again as though I did not already know that my breathing pattern was irregular.

"It sounds like you are experiencing a panic attack." She repeated.

"How. Do. You. Know. What. This. Is?" I whispered quietly as not to disturb the receptionist.

She went on to tell me about a family member who experienced a panic attack, and that my symptoms sounded similar.

I thought to myself, *"Why haven't I heard about this before now?"* I was stunned.

She explained that nobody in our family spoke about panic attacks.

By this time, my nerves were in an awful state of confusion. I was getting upset because I was experiencing something that others were familiar with, yet I was clueless.

I recall asking my sister for sound advice as to what to do about the panic attack. I do not remember her response, because at that moment my heart was pounding faster than the snare drum during a band competition. All I could think about was how to get out of there without anyone noticing me or before I passed out. By that time, I was undoubtedly gasping for air and panicking in the way that I suddenly understood panic!

Symptoms of a Panic Attack includes Hyperventilation, Sweating, Chest pain, Fearfulness and/or terror, Nausea, Cold chills or hot flashes, and Sense of impending doom. (www.nimh.org)

IT IS AN EMERGENCY

Although I was terrified about what was going on with my irregular breathing, I was equally ashamed. I did not know how to explain how I was feeling, and I refused to draw any attention to myself by having an ambulance arrive at my place of employment, so I called a taxi.

By the time I made it from the 49th floor to the lobby, there was a yellow taxi sitting out front waiting for me. Luckily, I was able to walk out of the building and get in the cab without anyone noticing.

When I arrived in the emergency room lobby, a technician took my blood pressure and checked my pulse rate. He quickly escorted me by wheelchair to a room where many other technicians were waiting. They hooked several wires to a machine and the others to my finger, chest, legs, and arms. At the time, I did not realize that this was going to be the first of many experiences with an EKG machine.

Once they removed all of the clamps from the square bandage-like tape, they took me to a room with one bed where I immediately fell asleep. I slept like a baby for a few minutes, but it felt like hours when someone tapped my shoulder. It was the emergency room doctor.

"How are you?"

"I feel great, actually!"

"Is everything okay at work? With your children? Your EKG came back, showing that your heart is excellent. Is everything okay at home?" He said as he flipped through the pages that were attached to the clipboard.

"Ye, ye, Yes! Ev, ev, ev, everything is fa, fa, fa, fine!" I suddenly burst into tears and surprisingly started stuttering as I responded.

"If everything is fine, why are you crying?" He said while he pulled two tissues from the small box next to my bed.

"I don't know?" I responded as I grabbed the tissue.

He scribbled notes on the papers that were attached to the clipboard, as I watched wondering, what is he going to do now that I started crying? He tore off a piece of paper and calmly said, *"Well, something must be wrong. Here is a prescription. Take these and see your family doctor."*

"What Just Happened? Fluoxetine? Really? I am not CRAZY! I do not need any medication. This prognosis doesn't make sense. I

really could not breathe. What does the change in my breathing pattern have to do with my mind? Why did he give me a pill that's usually recommended for crazy people? Every time you heard this certain name brand for fluoxetine it was associated with a person who had erratic behavior. Before my breathing pattern changed, I was functioning like an average person, minding my own business, and not bothering anyone or anything. I am a Christian; I am going to believe in God for my healing. I should trust God for the healing of my mind because that was just satan trying to confuse me. No one can ever know about what just happened."

These were only a few of the thoughts running through my mind as I went from one side of the house to another, cleaning it thoroughly. Cleaning was all I could do to keep from breaking down and crying profusely. All I could think about was: *"What would people say if they knew I was taking a crazy pill? What would they say if they found me dead from whatever was really causing my breathing pattern to change? If I am about to die, I need to clean up my house."* I found myself putting my jewelry in a visible location, next to my house and car keys. I thought to myself, *"If I became dizzy, confused or passed out, someone could easily find these things."*

The trip to the doctor and the diagnoses disturbed me so much that I was extremely confused. I was breathing correctly but my nerves were so bad that I was constantly worrying and wondering about what just happened. I was not convinced that my irregular breathing had anything to do with my mind. I knew something was not right, but I just could not put my finger on it and what the doctor was telling me was just not it!

Over twenty years ago, society persuaded me to believe that certain antidepressants were used to help people who had irrational behavior. Some people thought that these types of drugs did not cure you, but instead, caused the reaction. As I reflect, I was not ashamed of taking the prescription. I was more worried about what it would do to me and what people would say and think about me. *Antidepressants and other drugs like it are used for treating depression, bulimia, obsessive-compulsive disorder, panic disorder, and premenstrual dysphoric disorder.* Not all people use the same treatment options. Now that I know more about the benefits of antidepressants, I am glad that I am no longer ashamed. I hope you find the best treatment options for your situation.

WHAT IS PANIC DISORDER?

People with panic disorder have sudden and repeated attacks of fear that last for several minutes or longer. These are called panic attacks.

According to the National Institute of Mental Health, Panic disorder often begins in the late teens or early adulthood. More women than men have panic disorder. But not everyone who experiences panic attacks will develop panic disorder. (www.nimh.org)

2

NEARLY DIED

Most summers, my daughter traveled to Missouri to spend time with her cousins. This particular week, it was time for her to return home. My excitement was building. I knew that she'd have tattoos created by the sun using her lime green and black bathing suit as the stencil. This suntan signified that she spent time doing one of her favorite things, swimming.

The weather was ideal for a road trip. But for some reason, that day, I felt so tired that I could have fallen asleep standing up. I asked a friend to help me drive to Oklahoma, where we used a popular burger joint as our halfway marker for the trip between Texas and Missouri. To my surprise; this was a lifesaving decision. The engine to the car had not started before I drifted off to sleep. I slept the entire 10-hour journey to Oklahoma and back to Texas.

What started off to be an ordinary Friday afternoon, quickly transformed into a haunting night that changed my life forever. We arrived home safely after the drive from Oklahoma and prepared for bed. But then, I started feeling queasy, followed by vomiting and diarrhea. It was not unusual for me to contract a stomach virus, so I knew what medication to request from the doctor. *"I am throwing up and have diarrhea again. Would you please call in a prescription?"* I asked, while holding my head over the bathroom toilet. He honored my request with no hesitation.

Anticipating the next round of vomit, I remained hunched over the trash can while sitting on the edge of the bed. After calling the doctor, the puking and diarrhea continued. More fatigued than before, I could barely make it to the bathroom. That's when I decided to call a friend and asked him to pick up my medicine. I knew that I was unable to make it to the pharmacy because I could barely make it out of bed. By the time he arrived with the prescription, I had asked him to take me to the emergency room instead.

THE BLOOD

A trip to the emergency room for dehydration after a stomach virus was ordinary for me too. Once I arrived at the hospital, the nurses started IV fluids through my arm. Since I waited too long to treat my stomach virus, I ended up going to the emergency room to get fluids for dehydration. There they would add the nausea and diarrhea medications to my IV fluids. I started feeling better right away. After being discharged from the hospital, for a while, I tried to avoid eating food that could potentially cause nausea.

This time was different. When I arrived at the emergency room, I remember seeing John holding Lauren in his arms. *"I am losing my sight. I can't see you anymore,"* I said to him as the hospital staff approached me to catch me before I fell to the floor. I recall the nurse immediately sitting me in a wheelchair and racing me to a room where they began hooking me up to IV fluids. This time there were several technicians around me — one on each side. One was squeezing a bag of blood with his hands, and another one wrapped a blood pressure sleeve around the blood bag to force blood into my veins quicker. I lethargically looked at the nurse to my right and said, *"Please give me the fluids so I can go home."*

The last thing I remember was the technician looking at me and saying these words:

"If you would not have come in when you did, you would have (as he tilted his head to the side and closed his eyes) *died."*

The next day, I remember seeing my mom and several of my family members surrounding my hospital bed. It wasn't until the day after that I discovered that I had internal bleeding and lost several pints of blood due to a ruptured fallopian tube. This particular stomach ache resulted in the doctors performing emergency surgery. One reason I did not die was that my stomach was floating in the blood. As a result, the blood on my stomach caused me to be nauseous. Had I gone to sleep instead of going to the hospital, I would have died.

A NEW DISCOVERY

Looking back on how the experience began, I distinctly recall having a sharp pain in my lower abdomen that Wednesday. It was very sudden and left as quickly as it came. *"Oh, maybe it was just gas,"* I thought to myself. I suppose that the pain that occurred in my lower abdomen that Wednesday was my fallopian tube rupturing. The blood loss caused the severe fatigue that I was experiencing the days before.

Is it possible that this is where it all began-- the root cause of my panic attacks the trauma that caused me to worry about things that other people ignore? What I thought was a stomach virus was actually about to kill me.

My near-death experience is one of the reasons that I urge people not to be a physician for yourself. I almost died from internal bleeding that felt like a stomach virus. When I am nauseous, I often think about that day and wonder, *"Did my tubes burst again?"* If I think the worst, I panic. If I know what possibly caused nausea, I remain calm.

If I am bold, outspoken, and on fire for the Lord, my near-death experience has a lot to do with why! God allowed me to be here over thirty years later for a reason, and I want to show Him my gratitude by spreading the good news, that Jesus Christ is real and alive today. He allowed me to be here to tell you this story.

WHAT CAUSES PANIC DISORDER?

Panic disorder sometimes runs in families, but no one knows for sure why some family members have it while others do not. Some researchers have found that several parts of the brain, as well as biological processes, play a key role in fear and anxiety. Some researchers think that people with panic disorders misinterpret harmless bodily sensations as threats. By learning more about how the brain and body functions in people with panic disorder, scientists may be able to create better treatments. Researchers are also looking for ways in which stress and environmental factors may play a role. (www.nimh.org)

3

FORCED OUT

One hot summer in late August, just a few weeks after school started for most of Texas, someone broke into my house in the middle of the day. They came through a bedroom window by prying it open then simply sliding it up. Although, I had an alarm system, I did not have window sensors because the alarm company suggested glass break sensors. They recommended them because they said that most burglars break the window, unlatch the window, and then enter the home. In retrospect, I should have considered the worst-case scenario of someone silently prying the window open.

For several years, I slept in that bedroom not realizing how easy it was for someone to access my home without triggering the alarm. That experience left me with a strong sense of vulnerability. While thankful, at times I was still paranoid. What if they come back? What all do they know about my house? What else did they take?

These were just a few things that worried me about returning to my house. Having someone break in my home was another life-changing experience. I now have a real story, and this is not just something on the local news, this happened to me.

The first night after the break-in, I did not want to sleep at my house. I had a friend who lived nearby come home with me while I gathered a few of my things. I stayed at her home the first night, then a hotel the next few nights. I could not return to my house because I was petrified.

The recommendations for protecting my home started pouring in from purchasing a wooden toy slingshot to two trained German Shepherds. During this time, I was uncertain about my beliefs as it pertained to Christians owning a gun. Then someone whom I loved and respected said to me, *"Do you think Peter and the disciples had swords just to cut fish?"* I interpreted this as him saying, *"Get a gun!"*

All of the recommendations were taken into consideration as I desperately needed to feel safe again in my home. I changed my security alarm system; switched to a different monitoring company; installed additional security cameras; walked around my entire house praying and sprinkling olive oil (blessed oil) around the perimeters of my house; and purchased a taser. This break-in transformed my view about a lot of things, including that of owning a firearm. Although this was an extremely frightering experience, I thank God for His grace and protection for the many years that I lived there unharmed.

HELP!

I returned home after spending several dreadful days in a hotel, because my fear turned to frustration and anger. I was infuriated that the burglary kept me from sleeping at home. A few nights later, there was a noise outside of the front window. It appeared to be someone talking. Jumping out of bed, while grabbing my gun, I ran to the window to make sure that whatever was outside did not come inside.

Peeking through the blinds trying not to bend them too much, I watched and listened to the people talking. Then I flipped on the light switch near the front door while tightly holding my gun. Triggering the alarm on my car was something that I was taught to do to let people know that I was at home. So I pressed the panic button to activate the siren. As I clinched my gun, I was praying that I did not have to use it but thankful that I could protect myself if necessary. My heart started to beat rapidly. Though the rhythm of palpitations was the same as what I experienced while having a panic attack, my thought process was different. I knew what was causing the racing heart, so I knew what to do to calm my fear.

After checking all the locks on the doors and windows and pacing the floor for several minutes, I glanced out the front window again. This time I noticed people moving around the front of my house. Nevertheless, I hurried to my bedroom where my cell phone was on the charger, and called the police.

While the police checked the perimeter of my house, I called a friend to explain what was happening. We discussed how I was afraid to sleep alone at home so she invited me to spend the night with her. Although she lived an hour away, it did not matter. I just wanted to get one good night's sleep. I could have called my friend down the street again, but I was wondering if what I saw outside of my window was real or a panic attack. By this time, not only did I want to leave my house, I wanted to vacate the neighborhood.

The two female police officers who arrived at my home that night seemed very concerned and frustrated simultaneously. I asked them to walk me to my car. I surely felt I needed an escort by this time. One of them said to the other, *"Will you step outside so that I can have a moment alone with her?"*

She sat on my couch as close to me as possible without touching me and said, *"Don't let anyone run you out of your house.*

You have a gun. If someone comes in here, use it! They don't want you; they want your stuff."

I was tightly gripping my gun, and my tears were flowing, while my right leg was shaking like a toddler who had to pee. I suddenly became afraid of the officer. As she sternly looked in my eyes, she went on to say, *"Now we are going to walk you to your car tonight, but do not call us again."* Obviously, I had called them so many times that she knew that I needed help. But the help I needed was not from a police officer.

Sometimes, I reflect on that experience as to how my insight was different during the panic attack. I wonder if what I thought were people moving around was actually the wind blowing the tree limbs.

THE GET-AWAY

The entire ordeal was draining, physically, mentally, and emotionally. Nonetheless, I managed to find enough strength to cry for the entire trip to my friend's house. I briefly shared with her and her husband what caused me to be terrified enough to drive fifty miles in the middle of the night. I was so depleted. I could not wait to get in the bed where I immediately fell asleep, but not before checking to make sure the bedroom windows were secure.

FORGIVENESS AND FEAR

I believe fear and forgiveness have similar characteristics, and they both may influence a person's mental well-being. These two *"F"* words can keep a person in bondage. As **fear** caused me to leave my house after the break-in, similarly, a person can do one adverse thing to you that causes **forgiveness** to leave your heart.

What are **you** afraid of and why? This burglary helped me realize the impact and power of one bad memory, and how it can cause you to erase all of the pleasant memories. Of the many years that I lived in that home, one incident caused me never to want to live there again.

Who have **you** not forgiven, and why? Forgive yourself for whatever you have done in your past while on your journey to loving yourself. Only then, can you forgive others. We all know that everyone makes mistakes. So, the quicker you can forgive yourself and the people who have hurt you, the sooner you will find yourself recovering.

---

*And he looked up, and said, I see men as trees, walking.
After that he put his hands again upon his eyes, and made
him look up: and he was restored, and saw every man clearly.
(Mark 8:24-25)*

4

THIS MEANS WAR

One day after work, I was driving northbound on Central Expressway headed home when I noticed something irregular, or at least in my mind it seemed that way. I saw several white lines painting the blue sky that appeared to be smoke from the tail of an airplane. I did not see any planes, only the smoke-like lines in the air. These may have been simple white clouds, but that day, it appeared to be smoke. I instantly thought that the country was at war. I turned on my radio to listen for information on the news, but heard nothing but the same old updates. The speed limit on the freeway was 65, and we were barely moving. *"What is happening on this freeway?"* I whispered to myself in a panic. The eighteen-wheelers in front of me and in the right lane next to me made it impossible for me to see ahead.

My mind started racing. *"What am I going to do?"* I thought to myself. There is smoke in the air and there is a fire on the freeway. I went from assuming we were at war, to worrying that there was going to be a massive fire on the highway. Meanwhile, I was stuck behind this massive truck with nowhere to go. I knew that something was not right with my thought process. *"Enough is enough! I need to get help."* I recall calling a pastor with whom I finally became comfortable with sharing my experience.

"Hello Pastor, I am going through some strange things right now. I need to talk to someone."

He suggested that I schedule a meeting with one of the missionaries. As I am writing this story, his suggestion made perfect sense. But what I heard was, *"I don't have time for you!"* Back then, my perception was skewed because I was not well. I finally developed enough courage to share these strange things that were happening to me with someone, and he referred me to somebody that I have never spoken to before. No thank you! I will try to figure it out on my own. Maybe, he did not know how to help? Or perhaps he suffered from a mental illness too, and did not know what to say. These are things that I consider now, but then, I just felt abandoned.

TOUCH YOUR NEIGHBOR

As a young girl, I was either on my way to church, at church, or leaving church. Therefore, I learned about Jesus Christ very early. I was at church so much that I remember certain scriptures just because the preacher recited some of the same ones so often. Going to church was just my way of life. I never knew anything different.

My family was often one of the first to arrive for the evening church services. There were many times that my mom had to unlock the doors, turn on the lights, and even have us pick up trash from the prior service.

At the beginning of the service, we participated in Bible Drill contests for prizes, which was sometimes a voucher for candy from the church candy store.

On some Sunday afternoons, the children in our neighborhood gathered to play softball on the parking lot that was behind our house. The game ended when my siblings and I heard our mom calling us, saying, *"Come home, it is time to get ready for church!"*

One week in particular, we were having a revival! Do you hear about week-long revivals these days? We attended the revival every night. The service started with everyone kneeling for prayer. One person began praying until they became tired and then another person took over leading the prayer.

The prayer lasted for about an hour; then someone started singing, which was the signal that it was time to get up and participate in what was called *"Testimony Service."* Something else I don't hear about anymore. During Testimony Service, if you wanted to say something, you stood up or sang a congregational song to indicate that you wanted to give your testimony.

All of the testimonies started the same. *"First, I want to give praise to God, who is the head of my life, then I want to give honor to the pastor and his wife, the elders in the pulpit, the mothers and all the saints of God. I thank the Lord for finding me yet saved, sanctified, and filled with the Holy Ghost and fire. I do speak in tongues as the Spirit of the Lord gives utterance."* No matter what you said next, you ended by saying, *"Please pray for my strength in the Lord and that I hold on to be what He is calling me to be in these last and evil days."* This was one of the ways that we were taught at an early age to honor God and our elders.

After the evangelist preached his sermon, he asked, *"Does anybody want to give their life to Christ?"* If we took too long to go to the altar, he then asked if anybody wanted prayer. If no one answered, the evangelist or missionary walked through the aisle casing the pews randomly picking people to go to the altar.

Once you approached the altar, there were two, and sometimes three missionaries tarrying over you to help you receive the Holy Spirit. One repeatedly recited, *"Say thank you Jesus!"* The other two chimed in alternately saying, *"Give up to Him!"* and *"Hold on to Him!"* These phrases were things we giggled about often when we shared stories about church and revivals. *"How can we 'hold on' and 'let go' at the same time,"* we would say playfully.

On this Friday of the revival, I was that person who the evangelist selected to come to the front of the church. I had attended the revival every night that week and almost made it without being selected. The missionaries, tarried, telling me to *"give up to him, hold on, say thank you, Jesus,"* and this time I heard, *"You almost have **It**."* But I did not know what "**It**" was that I almost got. I just kept saying, *"thank you, Jesus, thank you, Jesus, thank you, Jesus"* until it sounded like, *"thank Jesus, thank Jesus, thank Jesus."*

THE HOLY SPIRIT

Apparently, this night something special happened, because this time I heard someone repeating, *"You have **It**. Baby, you got **It**!"*

Now I am SAVED, and I have ***It***!

I spent the entire weekend doing everything I was taught to do as someone who accepted Jesus Christ. But I still did not know what *It* was, that I had received.

The next Sunday during church, I passed a note to the pastor's wife. The note said, *"May I ask you a question?"* She held up her right hand with her index finger pointing towards the ceiling and tiptoed out of the church to meet me in the hallway near the silver water fountain. The fountain was a makeshift meeting place in the foyer of the church where everyone paused to chat or gossip while snatching a sip of water.

I began to explain to her that I kept hearing someone say that I have *It*, but I do not know what *It* is that I got! She said, *"Come on, let's go inside and tell the church what you just told me."*

She politely walked in the church, respectfully interrupted the pastor and whatever was going on and said, *"The baby has something to say."*

I stood in front of the entire church extremely nervous, not knowing what was about to happen.

*"Last Friday, when I was tarrying, they said I got **It**, but I do not know what I...."*

That was it! I collapsed onto the floor and began to speak in tongues. It was just like they said; it was flowing through my belly. I did not understand what I was saying, and I could not control what was coming out. I know that every time I tried to say thank you, Jesus, other words came out of my mouth like I was speaking a foreign language. I got **It**! I received the Holy Spirit by evidence of speaking in tongues as the Spirit of the Lord gave utterance.

And they were all filled with the Holy Ghost and began to speak with other tongues, as the Spirit gave them utterance. (Acts: 2:4)

Why am I telling you about my experience with salvation and the Holy Ghost? I am glad that you asked. I also think about how the church responded to my cry for help. I do not recall the church talking about mental illness. The closest they ever came to discuss mental affliction is when they referenced the scripture of the man that was cutting himself and was now clothed and in his right mind. But no one talked about mental illness from a clinical standpoint.

There were times that visitors came to church drunk, high, or perhaps with a mental illness. Mental activity was misunderstood; therefore, it was referred to as "spirits." I remember as a child hearing the minister urging us to stop playing and pray. *"Pray so these spirits will not jump out of them and into you."* Everything mental was turned into something spiritual or was used to measure your faith. Pray, read your Bible, stop worrying, trust God, etc. After a while, I was thinking that I was not praying enough; not praying correctly, or God was not hearing me. I felt if people knew that I was saved and depressed, they would judge me. They did and still do.

And they come to Jesus, and see him that was possessed with the devil, and had the legion, sitting, and clothed, and in his right mind: and they were afraid. (Mark 5:15)

GET READY FOR YOUR BLESSING

As time went by, I noticed a pattern. It seemed as though I received a blessing after each severe panic attack. Perhaps, the panic attack in 1997 was the storm before my blessing because a few months later I purchased my first home. To some, the homebuying process is overwhelming, but as a young single mother of two the entire process was seamless. Furthermore, the severity of the panic attacks made my fear of living alone seem like nothing. Now I expect a miracle or blessing after each panic attack.

Knowing this, I believe that there are times that we have adverse experiences in life, but we learn something from it that makes us wiser and stronger.

It is good for me that I have been afflicted; that I might learn thy statutes. (Psalm 119:71)

My mom and I talked about just about anything. It took me a while to get the nerve to discuss my struggles with panic attacks and taking the medication. Once I spoke about my concerns, she shared with me the scripture of the blind man who Jesus healed. *"Jesus healed him, but he still had to do something,"* she said. *"God created the doctors to help us, don't let the devil keep you from using what God has put in place to help you."* She encouraged me to take the prescribed medication and believe in God for my complete healing. *"Why go to the doctor if you are not going to do what they recommend?"* If the medication does not help, work with your doctor until you find out what is best for you. This conversation was the breakthrough that I needed. I was finally on the road to recovery.

When he had thus spoken, he spat on the ground, and made clay of the spittle, and he anointed the eyes of the blind man with the clay. (John 9:6)

HERE WE GO AGAIN

For several years, I was able to manage panic attacks without any medication, but during this time, I recall attending church more frequently. I believe that attending church and reading the Holy Bible is essential to mental health. The preachers shared motivating messages for people in despair. Each sermon seemed as though it was for me. I never wanted to miss a service, because I knew that I would hear more about how to deal with this thing called LIFE.

Several messages contributed to my healing process. One sermon I recall that helped me tremendously was a message about God parting the Red Sea so Moses could lead the Israelites out of Egypt to the Promised Land to escape Pharaoh and his army. I was famous for quoting scriptures, but now I was learning their meaning and how to apply them daily. I interpreted the passage as saying, *"Whatever is chasing you, God will part the sea for you to go through and close it so your enemy will drown and never bother you again."* It was something about this message that helped me to cope with my panic attacks for a while. Maybe I imagined my panic attacks and depression drowning like Pharaoh's army.

Like most things in life, nothing lasts forever. The messages changed, or I changed. Either way, the place I was seeking for hope and healing, was starting to become a place of hurt and pain.

Pharaoh's chariots and his host hath he cast into the sea: his chosen captains also are drowned in the Red Sea. (Exodus 15:4)

5

CRAZY OR NOT, HERE I COME!

My next attempt to get help was going to a counselor. The counselor seemed to be talking to me as though she was reading a teleprompter. They were still learning, and I felt as though I was a test subject. I thought they could use my information as a resource to help them with their database and quota. While I was speaking, the counselor was doing a lot of nodding and responding using safe words. I did not need safe words. I needed help!

Many people are still not comfortable with talking to counselors or psychiatrists. I believe that licensed professionals are better equipped now because there is more comprehensive training, education, information, and resources that was not available fifteen years ago. One way to counteract the fear of counselors is to promote awareness and encourage people like myself who once were discouraged in the past. It's essential to try different professional services until you find one that works. We also have to eliminate the shame by reminding people that a psychiatrist is a person who studied mental health, as a cardiologist study heart health. The stigma is valid because there are so many misconceptions. Perhaps, educating society about mental illness will cause more open discussions that will lead to the stigma vanishing altogether.

After spending three days staring at the ceiling, it was time for me to try seeing a counselor again. I was still not ready to see a psychiatrist. I was afraid, but at this point, what did I have to lose. I had lost peace, friends, family, job opportunities, and truly, my desire to be engaged with anyone or anything other than my bed.

As I drove into the parking lot, I parked in a spot close to the door. It was perfect because it was raining, and I had forgotten my umbrella. Maybe it slipped my mind as it required all of my strength and energy to take myself that day.

As I entered the building, I slowly opened the double glass doors while looking around to see if anyone was watching. I did not want anyone to recognize me or notice that I was going to a therapist. Then, I took the dreadful elevator ride to the second floor. When the bell rang and doors opened, I slowly walked off the elevator toward the entrance to the doctor's office. My legs were heavy as two steel beams. I was so nervous because I did not have a clue what to expect.

The reception area had a sign that said, PLEASE HAVE A SEAT. *"Great, that is one less person I have to talk to today."* I thought to myself. But before I could sit down, a lady came out from around the corner into the reception area.

"Hello, how may I help you?"

"I am Karen Metcalfe. I have an appointment today,"

"Great. Have a seat. I will be with you in 5 minutes. Would you like some water?" She asked as she checked my name off the sign-in sheet that was sitting on the desk.

"No, thank you. However, may I use your restroom," I replied. This was my chance to either get it together or escape and return to my cave at home.

Our counseling session started off outstanding. I think I started with when I was in kindergarten to avoid talking about what was happening that day. I figured by the time I started to discuss high school, my time would be up, and I would have escaped the conversation again.

Nevertheless, she had a sheet of paper that looked like a checklist of questions to ask me. We went through the list, but I did not get any clear-cut answers as to why I had panic attacks.

"How are you today?"

"Today, I am great! It's the days that I cannot get out of bed that I want to discuss." I thought to myself.

"I am fine," I replied.

The conversation became tough when she asked, *"What brings you here today?"*

"Where do I start?" I replied as I began to exhale because I was finally talking to someone who was *"supposed"* to listen to me.

"Oh, wait. I get it. The objective is to get me to come back for multiple visits." I am aware of my tendency to be analytical, therefore, I analyzed the session by thinking: If counselors provided all the information needed on my first visit, they would not continue to make a profit. With this philosophy, I did not feel that it was about me getting better right away but about the company making money. I understood it in theory, but today, I needed help. I needed answers. I did not want to go through multiple appointments to get what I

needed to survive. I was losing my mind and was not sure if I would live to make it back for another visit.

DISABILITY SCREENING

Finally, I had an appointment with a psychiatrist. Not because I wanted to, but because it was required. I assumed this person was appointed by the state to counsel mental illness patients. But their job was to screen individuals who applied for mental health disability.

"Count backwards, starting at 100, decreasing the number by 2."

Count backwards? What does this have to do with my panic attack? Really? That's when I knew that the meeting was not designed to address my immediate concerns about why I could not keep it together.

People often ignored my cry for help, so why should this time be different? Perhaps she is observing me today and thinking, *"There is nothing wrong with her, let's get through these forms so I can take my lunch break."* She stared in my eyes and nodded her head as if to say she understood my responses. *"But, am I wasting my time?"* I thought to myself as I tried to hold back the tears. *"Then again, I cannot blame her for treating me like I was just someone trying to take advantage of the disability system, because looking at me through the naked eye, maybe she thought I was fine."* Nevertheless, no two days are the same. If you interviewed me on one of my worst days it wouldn't be necessary to use your form to determine that my condition was debilitating.

She continued asking questions and marking my responses. My answers guided her to the next question. As the session concluded, she passed me a tissue and said, *"You should hear from someone within the next two weeks."*

This session was a rigorous workout for my emotions. I spent over fifty minutes crying or trying not to cry. I left feeling worse than I did before. I opened up to a stranger who will use my personal information like that of a lab rat so she can check the box that we met that day.

Here are a few things to consider that may help encourage mental health awareness.

1. Like a good hairdresser or barber, continue to

search for the licensed professional or support group that works best for you. *"Care more about how the inside of your head works, then how the outside of your head looks."*

2. Talk to the leader of your church about starting a mental health group session. There may be licensed professionals in your congregation who are willing to start a support group.

3. Talk to your employer about starting a support group and mental health awareness training.

Through researching and communicating with others about my struggles, I discovered a lot of helpful information. The National Institute of Mental Health's website is an excellent place to start.

6

DON'T PULL THE TRIGGER

L ike most young girls, I always dreamed of getting married, having children, and living in a house with a pretty white picket fence. So, I watched my mom cook, clean, sew and other duties that I would do someday as a wife and mother.

The magic began during my spectacular sophomore year of college. I strolled through the lunchroom to grab a quick bite to eat before heading to my next class. As I approached the food buffet, I could see the kitchen staff through the glass wall busy washing dishes and preparing meals. There he was, this tall, light-skinned, good-looking man. He was so handsome that I failed to notice the stinking odor coming from the grease, water, and food stains on his ugly brownish looking uniform. Long story short, ten years later, I gave birth to his son.

Suddenly, my life of endless bliss plunged. Roy was diagnosed with cancer in his early thirties. When he first told me that he had cancer, I was concerned, but not worried. *"No big deal, I thought to myself. My sister was diagnosed with cancer a few years prior. She survived, he will too."* These thoughts brought peace and hope to what in reality, was a horrible situation.

Also, I didn't know the severity of his sickness. I only knew of a few people who had cancer, and all of them survived. Unless it was someone who maybe had lung cancer from smoking or something like that, I understood it. Studies show that our habits contribute to our health, both good and bad. I was confident that he'd survive. He did not smoke. He drank plenty of water, exercised, and ate somewhat healthy. So, you could imagine my shock and disbelief when we discovered that he was sick. What happened next was nothing that any of us expected.

We were headed to church for Bible study. I remember exactly where I was standing when I received the call. *"Karen, this is Kate. Roy has passed."* As I fell to my knees, hitting the floor, I cried and exclaimed, *"What will happen to my son? How will I explain this to him?"* I could not imagine my life raising my son alone. There are days that I still do not believe it and even some nights that I dream he is still alive. Talk about going crazy, I thought I'd be somewhere picking cotton out of a mattress. When my son's father died, I was devastated, lost, scared, heartbroken, and confused.

Roy losing his battle with cancer was one of the most depressing seasons of my life. I lost faith in recovering from a sickness. I recalled thinking, something with the same symptoms as a stomach virus could have killed me. Now cancer took Roy's life. This caused illnesses to weigh heavier on me. A simple disease was more severe and a more severe condition, that some people survive, took Roy's life.

In 1979 my dad was hospitalized after having a stroke.

He never returned home, but my 96-year-old mom is still living after having a stroke over thirty years ago. I pray and try to believe, but I can't help but think about these events and worry or sometimes think the worst.

Several days after Roy's death, my college roommate called to comfort me. *"Karen, I'm on my way to pick you up. You should get away from everything for a while."* She said while listening to my grief-stricken voice over the phone. When we arrived at her home, she did her best to comfort me. I recall sitting on her couch, but I could not rest. My body was shaking uncontrollably like the ground during an earthquake.

Roy's death caused my serotonin levels to drop drastically. As a result, I was rushed to the emergency room several times a month because my heart was beating out of control. Each time the doctors checked my blood pressure, they noticed my resting heart rate escalated to over one hundred and thirty beats a minute. The nurses provided a wheelchair and hurriedly took me to a room. Then they administered medication through an IV. His death accelerated my fear of separation, loss, sickness, and death; just the complete horror of the unknowns. Although I have faith, I am apprehensive to believe that illness of any nature will have a favorable outcome. I often wonder if this is the reason that loss triggers my panic attacks.

ASHAMED TO GO

One evening, I was resting in bed watching television. Suddenly, I noticed that my left thumb was cramping and moving back and forth by itself like a joy stick on a game controller. *"What is going on?"* I thought to myself. I massaged it. Then I held it under the bathroom faucet while running cold water on it. But nothing I tried seemed to work. Now I was worrying that I was having a stroke. My heart raced for over an hour. My thumb continued to throb while I dressed to go to the ER. By then, my racing heart and thumb were competing for attention. This time, I drove to a different hospital because I was too embarrassed to visit the same emergency room. I was afraid that the staff would say, *"Here she comes again."* The lady with the panic attacks. Or worse, *"Here comes the crazy lady."*

During one panic attack, I drove to the fire station because I was too embarrassed to go to the hospital once again. My left eye swelled shut and puffed up like a golf ball had been implanted under my skin. My heart began to beat rapidly. I worried that I was having an aneurism because I recalled this being a symptom for someone else. It turned out to be an allergic reaction to a dog.

The pain in my thumb was real and my eye was literally swollen shut. These events caused me to have progressive panic attacks because I did not know the root cause of the pain. I used the term *"progressive"* because there were times that I had sudden rapid heartbeats, and I was able to manage the panic attack by drinking cold water, using breathing techniques, taking a nap, or taking my medication. However, I had to go to the emergency room to stabilize my heart rate for what I refer to as a progressive panic attack.

JUST MY IMAGINATION

Have you ever had anyone tell you that they had illusions that caused their panic attack? No one ever told me, nor did I care to discuss my experiences. The illusions were sudden and had random symptoms so I never related the event to a form of a panic attack until later.

These were events where I did not have to rush to the hospital due to a sudden onset of fear which caused my heart rate to increase, but rather the illusion started first, then the rapid heartbeat followed. If I heard news of someone having a heart attack, then something would happen to me physically to make me think I was having one. Then my heart started to beat fast and loud enough to hear without a stethoscope.

Once I heard about someone who had breast cancer. During this time, we did not have the Internet and other resources that we have today. I recall stepping out of the shower like usual, walking towards my double sinks and standing in front of the mirror to dry off. This time, I noticed something that I did not recall seeing before. My breast had dark black circles around the nipples. I panicked. *"Oh no, something is wrong with my breast."* I thought to myself. I could not remember how a breast was supposed to look. I recall looking for a pamphlet that demonstrated how to check yourself for breast cancer. I was too embarrassed to tell anyone about this experience. Honestly, I am not at all enthusiastic about sharing this with you in my book, but I am hopeful my transparency will help someone with their struggles. Back then, I did not say anything for several reasons. The main reason was because I was afraid that I would be committed to a hospital, and would no longer be able to raise my children. So...I was silent!

Another illusion occurred one morning while getting dressed for work. This time when I looked in the mirror, my forehead appeared to be larger, so I freaked out and thought that I had a brain tumor. Once I finished vomiting, I laid down. I felt much better after a nap. NOW, I am wondering if there was something wrong with that mirror.

These incidents did not cause me to have the panic attacks in the way that I experienced them in the beginning. The events had at least two things in common, the events caused a rapid heartbeat and I thought I was going to die.

I was encouraged to watch the movie *"A Beautiful Mind"* by Sylvia Nasar. This movie is a true story of the life of John Nash a thirty-year-old mathematician. Now known as *"John Nash the paranoid schizophrenic"*. Like Nash, I found myself on a painful, lonely journey of self-discovery. This movie helped to change my life. His story is not my story but close enough.

I often share things with my mom because she is a secret keeper. She prays for me, and always has a scripture ready for me. We memorized and studied the fourth division of Psalms. We recited it during some of my toughest times.

I recall her telling me that satan is nothing but a liar. Satan knows that he cannot touch me, so he messes with my mind. Satan is trying to keep me from telling the world about Jesus. If he can get my mind, I will be depressed and silent.

CHILDHOOD MEMORIES

My kindergarten teacher taught me to read, write, and identify the primary colors by cutting out leaves using construction paper. *"Red, yellow, orange, green, purple, blue, brown and black."* I often sang to myself as I placed the crayon neatly in the box with the name of the color facing up. I remember each time we used our crayons, I made sure that I organized them in the same sequence that my teacher pinned the leaves on the bulletin board behind her desk. Still, to this day, I organize things using this format, from clothes to shoes and accessories.

In the same way that colors trigger my memory about the bulletin board in kindergarten, I often wonder if seeing a suspicious person in a convenient store heightens my anxiety. When I was around three years of age, my mom, my older brother and I were shopping in a convenience store. All of a sudden, a man with a gun demanded that we all go downstairs into the basement while he robbed the store.

I often wonder if this is why, I occasionally abandon my merchandise and leave a store because someone who has a similar physique, voice, or walk, cause the memory to resurface. I often wondered if it was possible to erase my recollection of the robbery and sustain the memory of the colors. Perhaps I wouldn't have panic attacks when I am in a store.

We may never know why a person responds to the vicissitudes of life differently. But we should all agree that events from our past, either positive or negative, play a significant role in who we are today. We should not judge people because we will never know their entire story.

TRICKS ARE NOT JUST FOR KIDS

Being a victim of bullying as an adult triggered my depression and caused me to have several panic attacks. Although the bullying started when I was a teenager, I did not have panic attacks until my late twenties or early thirties. As a young teen, I recall leaving school early because one of my classmates had threatened to fight me after school. However, my dad sent me right back to school to stand up to the bully. As I made this five-mile hike back, I could barely see through the tears puddling in my eyes. The closer I made it, the heavier the tears became. At first, I was angry at my dad for making me walk back to school, but then I became angry at my bully for making me face my dad. I was so upset that now I was ready if I had to fight.

Perhaps this is why I continue to persevere and cry through any opposition. He taught me not to run from my problems and how to defend myself. I will talk more about bullying on my blogs, website, and maybe in my next book.

My life being a victim of bullying as a child and an adult is a book by itself. *Bullying – These Tricks Are Not Just for Kids©*

Because I was unable to pinpoint what triggered every panic attack, I cannot overemphasize the importance of receiving proper diagnosis and treatment. Consulting with a professional may help you identify your triggers so that you may ultimately have a better quality of life.

IS IT SOMETHING YOU ATE?

To this day, I do not know what it is about the food at one of my favorite restaurants that caused me to have mild panic attacks. They serve the best spinach dip, so I often ordered the dip with chips. But minutes after I ate it, my heart began to race. This restaurant was one of my favorite restaurants to visit with Roy. I do not know if the memory of going there with him had anything to do with my sudden attacks or not.

Let's fast forward to 2019 when I was in Chicago and I ate a hamburger from a well-known restaurant. I started to feel nauseous, then began having a panic attack.

Thankfully, I was with my daughter when this happened. *"Mommy, are you okay?"* She asked as she noticed me sweating and shaking. *"No, I am not. I am having a panic attack."* I said while nervously making my way to the bathroom just in case I needed to puke.

She offered me a bottle of cold water and pulled back the covers on the guestroom bed. I dozed off into a light sleep. I could hear the bedroom door squeak as she peeked in the room to check on me several times throughout the night. This attention to my wellbeing contributed to my speedy recovery from this panic attack. The next day, other than being more careful about my food selection, I went on about my day as though nothing happened.

I am not sure if it was something in the food that caused me to be sick, so I had a panic attack, or if the food caused the panic attack, so I became ill. Most times, the symptoms happen so quickly; it is hard to tell what happened first. Incidents like this and the one I experienced at these popular restaurants make me wonder if the influx of panic attacks and panic disorder has anything to do with the food we eat.

I am not and most likely will never be a vegetarian because I like baked chicken, fried chicken, chicken salad...okay, you get it. But I am convinced that there is something in the meat and other foods we eat that contribute to our mental health. Several articles on various websites suggest that certain foods may be a contributing factor in panic attacks.

Are There Foods That Cause Panic Disorder?

Eating disorders commonly co-occur with anxiety disorders. For those who have an anxiety disorder, a co-occurring eating disorder may make their symptoms worse and recovery more difficult. It's essential to be treated for both disorders. (www.adaa.org)

Triggers vs. Causes

What causes panic attacks is different from what triggers panic attacks. For example, my near-death experience may be the root cause of my panic attacks, but attending a funeral or hearing about someone's sickness or death are triggers of some of the attacks. While recently, other events have prompted my panic attacks, I strongly believe that hearing about someone's terminal illness and death are my main triggers.

There were times that I suffered from panic attacks, days or even weeks after attending a funeral. My involvement with a funeral, association to the person, age of the person, and cause of death determined the intensity of my worry. Even if I did not attend a funeral, I had mild panic attacks. If a knew of a person who died of something sudden like a heart attack, stroke, car accident, or aneurism I worried that something would happen to me.

If the person was older or self-inflicted, I tended to be able to handle that better. But I still could not bear to watch others grieve.

Sometimes being around a person who recently lost a loved one was hard. They had support to help get them through their journey. However, I returned home and suffered from panic attacks and depression and wouldn't tell anybody. Losing over thirty close family members and friends, caused me to empathize with others.

Sometimes, when I have a panic attack, I am not thinking of anything in particular. Often, a sudden rapid heartbeat has awakened me, but I do not recall dreaming of anything that caused the panic attack.

Studies show that genetics may **cause** a person's panic disorder, but not all family members have the disease. It may skip generations or family members. These are some things to consider: While one family member may suffer others may not. So they dismiss the sickness of the family member that struggles. Maybe because they do not understand what that person is really experiencing. You often hear in some communities, *"What goes on in this house stays in this house."* What if disclosing your illness will prompt people to wonder about theirs? Is it possible that sharing this information would help them and others that you may meet? Communication is essential to help clarify misconceptions so that we may all understand the causes, triggers and remedies to manage mental illness.

7

MISSING PERSON

Have you ever been in a crowded room, yet you felt alone? What is wrong with someone wanting to be accepted? Even the Bible says that it is not good for man to be alone. But why am I alone? This may not be the usual interpretation for this verse, it's just the version in my head.

The LORD God said, it is not good for the man to be alone. I will make a helper suitable for him. (Genesis 2:8)

As a young girl, not yet a teenager, I remember writing a note and placing it in a discreet place so that my father would find it. The note said: *"Don't Nobody Like Me."*

I made sure that my dad was in another room before placing the note where he could find it, but not see me put it there. I needed time to get to my hiding place before he discovered it. Not too much time, though, because I was too scared to be alone for an extended period. You can almost say; it was my own game of *"hide and seek."*

We lived in a 1940's style red brick 3-story home with a basement, seven bedrooms, and six other rooms where I could hide. I snuck upstairs to the third floor to hide under one of my brothers' beds, where I waited until my dad found me. I was too afraid to run away from home. I just wanted to know what they would do or think if they knew I was no longer there. I knew what it felt like to be without them because I felt alone daily.

"I wonder if my dad and siblings would miss me if I was no longer around." I thought to myself as I scrambled to my hiding place. I realize people commit suicide for different reasons. However, I never wanted to commit suicide. I

just wanted to be understood, respected, appreciated and loved.

The note was written to my dad because I wanted his attention. Something that I felt the others already received. Perhaps to everyone else, I received plenty of attention, but maybe it just wasn't enough attention for me. They were the babies of the family, or everyone else was much older. So that left me in a category all alone. I recall hearing things like *"Shut-up! You talk too loud! You can't go with them because you are too young."* And I felt that my younger sister and brother got away with some things that I did not, because *"I was old enough to know better!"*

When I heard my siblings yelling my name, I held my breath. Once they made it to the third floor, I pretended as if I did not hear them, simply because I wanted my dad to find me. *"Boochie. Boochie. Boochie. "Where are you?"* Once he found me, I was no longer a missing person. I received enough attention. However, it wasn't long before I went missing again…so I'd write another note.

One Sunday, I waited until my younger sister and brother

dressed for church. I eased my way into my parents' room, where my dad was comfortably sitting in his recliner watching television. It was two days after my breast surgery, therefore, I had something to help me with the case I was about to present to my dad. My goal was to be able to stay home alone with him while the others went to church. Although the surgery was an out-patient surgery, I was about to treat it like it was major one. I needed all the ammunition I could find because my mother was a tough person to crack when it came to attending church.

Originally one small lump was discovered on my breast, but during surgery, they found two and removed them both. I tried to use the operation as an excuse to stay home from church. My dad did not attend church, but he supported my mother's decision to make us go. Often, for the night services, I was able to avoid going to church. I persuaded my dad to let me stay home by massaging his Telly Savalas (Kojak) head.

He sat in his dark brown leather reclining rocking chair that was held together in certain places with gray duct tape. I waited until my mother would leave their large bedroom then I'd start massaging my dad's soft, wrinkled, bald-head. My mom would come in the room and exclaim, *"Boochie, why aren't you upstairs getting ready for church?"*

By now, my dad was relaxed watching Sanford and Sons while enjoying his head massage. He responded to my mother on my behalf in his stern deep voice, *"Let her stay home with me tonight!"* I tucked my chin in my chest to keep my mom from seeing the smirk I had on my face. *"Yes! I get to stay home."* I was allowed to stay home, but my mom gave me a list of chores that kept me so busy that the next time, I would think twice before pulling a stunt like that one.

I was a few years older than the baby sister and baby brother of the siblings. Everyone else was much older. I did not have a *"unique"* category. As I look back, the song *"Don't Nobody Like Me"* was a manner in which my siblings teased me. I am not upset because a song was written to tease me about the note. But I am wondering why nothing was done to see why I wrote the note in the first place. That may have been a good time for someone to see what was going on with me. But instead, my baby brother composed a song.

I never really thought about the impact the song had on me until I started this journey of self-discovery. Sometimes, I sang along with my siblings. It wasn't the song that bothered me. The real question was, why did I write the note, *"Don't nobody like me."* The song reminds me that I may have felt alienated and distant from people all of my life.

Even today, there are times that I feel distant from some of my siblings. *"They don't understand me."* I believe they love me, but don't like me, because I am different! My mom once told me, *"Boochie, you may often find yourself alone because where God is taking you, people will not understand. Some people don't have anything, and if you let them, they will cause you to lose everything you have or prevent you from growing."* These words were encouraging and painful to receive at the same time. Yet, I hold on to my mom's words of wisdom to get me through some of my darkest and loneliest days.

"If the world hates you, ye know that it hated me before it hated you.

If ye were of the world, the world would love his own: but because ye are not of the world, but I have chosen you out of the world, therefore the world hateth you.

Remember the word that I said unto you, the servant is not greater than his lord. If they have persecuted me, they will also persecute you; if they have kept my saying, they will keep yours also." (John 15:18-20)

8

FAMILY SECRETS

We were in a small dark room waiting for the nurse to call my mom's name for x-rays. I was standing next to my mom's hospital bed when I received a video call. The cell phone reception was intermittent, and there was very little room to move around with no privacy. But I had to take this call. It was my daughter. *"Mommy, I think I'm having a panic attack,"* she said. *"Where are you?"* I asked. I was trying to stand as still as possible to keep from losing the phone signal. *"My colleague is driving me to the emergency room,"* she replied. Listening to her trembling voice and imagining the look on her face was like looking in a mirror. *"May I speak with him."* I asked in a very calm voice.

Because I shared my personal experience with my daughter, she was able to recognize what was happening to her. I began talking to her colleague. I shared ways he could help her and prepared him for some things to expect when they arrived in the emergency room.

"Scott, thank you for driving her to the hospital. I want to let you know that when you arrive, she may not want to get out of the car."

I knew this because it happened to me a few times. I attempted to drive to the hospital many times. However, once I knew that I was close to a medical facility, I felt safe and my panic attack would subside.

Between the two of us, we were able to help my daughter manage her panic attack. She was able to return to her day-to-day responsibilities. Unlike me, she was able to avoid the costly emergency room visit because she did not have to suffer in silence.

One time, I was enjoying a meal with friends and family and encountered a panic attack. Several years ago, I remember walking through the grocery store shopping and had to grab a bottle of water off the shelf because my heart suddenly started to race. These events reassured me that it was crucial to share what my life was like as I experienced random attacks daily.

Conversations with my children are ongoing because with each panic attack or bout with depression, I learn something new. Each child is different, so it is up to you to decide what and when to tell them. I believe it is helpful to talk to my children because not only are they able to help me, I can now help them. Consequently, we can help others that we come in contact with daily.

I watched them work hard to avoid situations and activities that would have caused me additional stress and worry as a result of their lifestyles. They made many sacrifices because they did not like to see mommy sick. There were places that they did not go because they knew I would worry. There were television shows and movies that they would not watch because they knew that I could have an adverse reaction to the movie or show, days or weeks later.

Although, they spent several late nights and early mornings driving me to and from the hospital, when I think about it, my children never complained. They waited patiently in the hospital waiting area. Often when I returned to the lobby after treatment, they were both asleep. My daughter was sleeping in a chair, with my son's head laying in her lap. By this time, the lobby was vacant. Most of the patients and families were already treated and released or in rooms.

I want to encourage you to share ways with the people closest to you on how they may be able to help you cope with your mental illness. Be transparent about how you feel during a panic attack and depression. Things like, *"Get over it! You worry too much! It's no big deal!"* are a few things that I did not want to hear. Each person is different, therefore, it's important to share your preferences. Some people may be trying to help, but inadvertently saying the wrong thing could potentially make it worse. Instead, my suggestion to my children was to remind me that I would be okay. More importantly, I asked them to pray for me. It was essential that they allowed me to sleep. Sometimes, I preferred laying on a sturdy floor. If I laid in bed, my trembling body would cause the bed to shake which only made things worse. One thing I knew for sure was I did not want them to leave me alone.

A PAINFUL DISCOVERY

One day I decided to call my sister to check on her. I recall a time when I was concerned and depressed about my sister's battle with renal failure. I was often sad about it, but I did not say much. She was on an airplane headed to a women's conference with her church. That made me feel so much better to know that some people who deal with certain illnesses will fight through them and keep moving. My sister's determination to not allow her illness to prevent her from living her life gave me hope and peace to get through my day.

I believe losing my sister in 2007 was life-changing. It did not destroy my faith in God, but it has forever disturbed my peace. She made everyone feel as though they were her favorite. But I knew that I was the real favorite. After all, she gave me my nickname. I accredit her for things like my piano lessons, my first pair of *new* bell-bottom blue jeans, and my driving school classes. Like me, she was a middle child between two sisters. She understood me. She was like a mother to me and I was her *"Boochie Baby."*

I vividly remember the day I watched her go to sleep for the very last time. She responded to me, knew who I was, and she knew what was about to happen to her. I remember asking her if this was what she wanted. She had a tube in her mouth that I later realized was the only thing that was keeping her alive. So, she responded by nodding her head, *"Yes!"* I recall her telling me once before; that there were days that her body would hurt all over. I remember the doctor entering her room to give her a shot and I watched as he removed the tubes from her mouth. She requested to see my mom. Then she went to sleep. I had never watched anyone die before. Today, July 2019, is the first time that I thought about it that way. I never wanted to accept that I watched her die. I always referenced her death by saying, *"When my sister went to sleep…"*

My siblings and I rarely talked about what had occurred. For years, it seemed as though we avoided saying her name. I do not recall my siblings having any memorials. Peg's passing was an extremely sensitive and difficult subject. It was extra difficult for me because, I returned to Texas alone; while they still had each other.

One day, my daughter and I were discussing my response to Peg's death. She said, *"Mommy, you don't handle death well at all."* She went on to tell me that I had a drastic personality change after Roy's and Peg's passing. She shared that I began to drink, cut my hair and was just not myself. To this day, it baffles me that I am able to recall cutting my hair, but still do not remember any drinking. *"You were just not the mommy I once knew,"* She said.

Like some other illnesses, studies show that genetics may cause a person's panic disorder. But not all family members have it. I like to continue to make this point because of the misconception that individuals who have a mental illness caused it themselves. Panic disorder may skip generations or family members. These are some things to consider: While one family member may suffer others may not, so they do not understand what a person is going through. Therefore, they dismiss their sickness. You often hear in some communities, *"What goes on in this house stays in this house."* What if disclosing your illness will prompt people to wonder about theirs?

Also, they think they can fix it with the following steps: No more worrying, stop overthinking things, pray, and study your Bible. I am a firm believer that Jesus is a healer because people have been, will be, and can be healed from their mental illness or any disease for that matter. Yet, mental illness is not just what YOU think! There is NOT a switch we can use to turn it on and off.

9

REMOVING THE MASK

As I was headed home from work driving down the freeway, I could remember both of my arms in pain. The pain was so severe, it felt like my arms were between the jaws of an angry shark. I made several attempts to adjust my arms, alternately taking one arm off the steering wheel at a time to see if it would make a difference. But nothing changed; instead, it was only more painful.

"What is going on?" I wondered to myself while slowing down where now I was driving ten miles under the speed

75

limit. I remembered seeing a commercial that talked about the different signs of a heart attack for women. *"Am I having a heart attack?"* I thought to myself.

From this incident, I concluded that I could not watch certain commercials. What I hear and see severely affects how I think and respond to everyday life. If a commercial ask questions, *"Are you tired all the time? Do you find yourself..."* I immediately started checking off the boxes in my head and drawing the conclusion that I have the symptoms previously mentioned. So clearly, I must see my doctor or purchase the prescription for everything they are describing.

The adverse reaction also helped me realize that I cannot watch certain television shows or movies. Whatever is happening in the film, I sometimes imagine it happening to me. I may have a panic attack days or weeks afterward from going over the thoughts in my head over and over again. I am convinced that what you see and hear has a powerful impact on what you think, which causes you to be depressed or have a panic attack. Pastor John Haggi once said, *"Sometimes the best thing on the television is the knob to turn it off."*

By now, my children have moved away. I had to turn to my friends for help. So that day, I called a friend. I explained to her what was happening to me. The mask was removed! I asked if she would meet me at the emergency clinic that was close to my route home, just in case I needed someone to drive me home.

When I arrived at the clinic, the staff treated me like I was a drug addict looking for a fix. They did nothing other than check my blood pressure and place me in a room where I waited for over an hour. The nurse returned with some paperwork for me to complete and told me to schedule an appointment with my primary care doctor. But they billed me like they had performed major surgery.

After they released me, my friend and I were standing in the clinic parking lot. I was still a little shaky, but strangely, my arms were no longer in pain. She asked me what happened and if I needed a ride home. I recall telling her, I had finally figured out this panic attack thing. Although I did not know what caused the pain in my arms, one pattern

I began to notice is that after each panic attack, there was a significant life event. Low and behold, one month later, this panic attack was followed by me selling my house of twenty-one years.

ENOUGH IS ENOUGH!

For three long dark days, I laid on my smoked gray leather couch. The law of gravity justified my desire not to move. As I stared at the ceiling, the blades on the ceiling fan were spinning like my life. The chains hanging from the fan were rattling in the same matter that my body shook during a significant panic attack. But I did not have a panic attack. I was suffering from depression. As I sat staring at the ceiling wondering, why am I here? *"What just happened?"* I asked myself. *"Why can't I think straight? Why can't I handle this situation?"* I asked myself several questions trying to figure out what was going on with me. I played several movies and scenarios in my mind, but nothing made sense. I went down my phone book in my head thinking of someone to call. *"People have their own problems. They don't have the time or energy to deal with mine,"* I said as I tried to reason with myself. I often say that people could only advise you based on the information that you give them. I could not articulate some of the things to anyone else because I could not figure it out myself.

Often when people commit suicide. We say we did not know. What are some of the signs? If you notice someone who you have known for years start to do things out of the ordinary, is that a sign? If a person begins to isolate himself or herself, is that a sign?

What about the signs of depression? If a person who is known to be reasonably healthy starts to gain weight and let themselves go; there is no known evidence of a sickness or injury that is causing this change in their weight or appearance, is that a sign?

The more we talk about it, the more we will know. I was displaying signs daily of my depression, but either people did not want to believe me, had their own problems, or did not care. What should you do if you know that someone is depressed or suicidal?

I met a young lady who shared a story about her close

friend who attempted suicide. She said that she never knew her friend was suicidal. But as we were talking, she looked back and realized there were several signs. Society does not teach us the signs or what to do. It is taboo until something tragic happens.

DOG ON IT!

If it were not for my Golden Doodle, Har-V, whimpering to eat and go out to pee, I would have stayed on that smoked gray leather couch forever. I even thought about locking Har-V in the garage so that I could lock myself in the house and not answer the door or telephones. *"Good. Har-V took a dump. I do not have to get up from this spot again until tomorrow morning to take him outside again."*

It was Har-V's hazel brown eyes and innocent looking face that kept me from going to that extreme. It was as if he knew something was wrong because he would find a way to lay his head on my leg just to let me know that he was there for me. My routine for those three days was the same. Get up. Take the dog out. Feed him. Stare at the ceiling. Get up. Take the dog out again. Feed him. Stare at the ceiling until I fell asleep. There are times that I find having a dog could be challenging, costly and hard work, but it was times like those that let me know the value of having a service animal.

Whenever I could get out of bed and walk, he was always ready to walk with me. Sometimes it helped just hearing him breathe and snore as he slept close to me. Har-V was the one thing that was the same daily. The only thing I could count on not hurting me. He would just lay as close to me as he could because he knew I did not want him on the bed or couch. But when I was at my lowest, he ignored my house rules and reassured me that things would be okay by placing his head on my lap or leg. My house rules for a dog no longer mattered.

Having a dog has proven to me to be very helpful with my recovery from depression. I walked Har-V twice a day. There were times that I cried the entire time, but I kept walking. Movement is essential to a person who suffers from depression, and having a dog will force you to get up and go outside daily.

Breaking Point

Day three, there I was, in the same place looking at this same ceiling, but something was different. The fan was not moving. It was as though the switch had been flicked to turn off the fan. Likewise, a switch went off in my head. *"Wait a minute! Today, I am healthy! I have food to eat. I have clothes to wear. I have paid my bills and I am employed. I am not dead yet! What is the worst thing that could happen?"* I thought to myself. I finally learned what it meant to live one day at a time.

I realized that the only thing keeping me from being free was fear! Fear of failure. But who would I be failing? If I did not get out of this hostile situation, I was going to die. It was much too much for me to handle. God told me that He would not put more on me than I could manage. Was I at my max? Was I holding on to something out of fear?

Leaving my job and publicly talking about mental illness was the real test for me to see just how much faith I had. That day, I rolled off the couch, leaving my body print as a reminder that I had laid there much too long. I went upstairs, for the first time in three days. I took a shower, and put on fresh, clean clothes. I decided I was GOING TO LIVE ONE DAY AT A TIME. I WILL ONLY CONCERN MYSELF WITH WHAT IS GOING ON TODAY. I CANNOT AND WILL NOT WORRY ABOUT TOMORROW.

"Take therefore no thought for the morrow: for the morrow shall take thought for the things of itself. Sufficient unto the day is the evil thereof. (Matthew 6:34)"

CRIME SCENE

Those three days had a more significant impact on my life than I realized. During my doctor's visit, I noticed a drastic change in my weight. I struggled with my weight all of my life, but I managed to lose close to fifteen pounds in just three days. *"Not my ideal weight loss program, but at least I got something out of it."* I thought to myself trying to bring myself some happiness from all the doom and gloom that I had been facing.

When I returned to the scene of the crime, nothing there had changed, but I had changed. While taking a sip of my coffee, I heard God say, *"hang in there, this is all a part of the process."* I was so thrilled because this was the first time that I was able to smile in a long time. I was grateful to hear God talking to me amidst the chaos.

A few weeks later, I was resting on the couch. I guess you figured by now that this smoked gray couch is very comfortable. Anyway, I thought I was okay. I thought I had conquered this thing called panic attacks. I decided to make a significant life change. The need to use the bathroom awakened me. But something else happened.

My heart was racing as fast as a rabbit and as loud as a school band's drumline. I was furious. I knew I had made the right decision. Why was I experiencing a panic attack? I had no one to call. It was time for school to start, the people who I usually relied on were out of town or taking their children to school. I had to figure this one out by myself.

I slowly got up, retrieved a bottle of cold water from the refrigerator, took my medication, and made a mental declaration:

"I will no longer suffer from panic attacks alone. I will tell my

story about panic attacks and depression to help others. I am thankful that I know Christ and that I have a sound support system, but what about that person who does not know the Lord and Savior Jesus Christ? What about that person who does not know their value or worth? What about that person who does not have a support group? I promised God on that day that I would share my story to help others. If I can save one life; if I could encourage one person to accept Jesus Christ as his or her Lord and Savior; or if I can help one person manage or overcome panic attacks, it is worth it."

THIS TIME IT WAS NOT ME

Her facial expressions rotated like a traffic signal from a smile, to a blank stare, then to a frown. As I shared my story, the nodding head; the tears gathering in the eyes, and the changes in the facial expressions said it all. *"This time, it was not me. She is a Missing Person too."* I thought to myself.

Now that I have been talking about my journey, I can identify with others who struggle with depression and panic attacks. I think that this may be the reason some people avoid me. Maybe, some people do not want anyone to discover that they are missing.

Finally! I found other people who understand what my

panic attacks and depression were doing to me mentally, emotionally, socially, spiritually, physically, and financially.

These individuals, sound, and act just like me. However, we are different races, genders, religions, social classes, nationalities, and more. I tried to hold back my tears as I shared my experience.

Mental illness is something we have; yet, it does not define us! I received confirmation that I was sharing my story to tell her story.

There is someone who you can talk to about your sickness. You do not have to share your story with the world, but please share it with someone.

Are you a **Missing Person?**

10

THE SYSTEM

It was three days before Thanksgiving. Most people were planning dinner, packing for travel, and spending time with friends and family. As I parked my car in front of the one-story white brick building, I carefully looked for a sign to make sure that I was at the correct address. Slowly walking along the long sidewalk towards the front door, I couldn't help but see my reflection in the large square shaded windows that lined the building wondering, who was that person and why is she here?

Upon entering the building, there were people of all

ages, races, and nationalities throughout the large waiting area. Some were barely moving around the room using walkers, canes, and wheelchairs. While others, like me, did not have a visible condition that justified being at the Social Security Office for Disability Benefits.

There were several rows of gray chairs with silver legs lined side by side in the center of the lobby. There were additional chairs lined up around the walls and along the inside of the windows. Nonetheless, there were still more people than chairs. There were also two fully armed security officers visibly present. One officer was sitting in a chair. The other one was assisting an elderly lady in a wheelchair operate the computerized sign-in system located on the wall next to his desk.

As I approached the desk, I noticed a monitor on the wall that said, *"NOW SERVING NUMBER 117."*

"May I help you?" One of the officer's asked as I approached the desk.

The officer assisted me with registering using the

electronic sign-in station, then told me to have a seat until my number was called. While sitting in the lobby, I experienced all forms of anxiety, frustrations and fears. *"This atmosphere is trying my patience. Please make this child stop yelling. But how can I be so insensitive? What if the child was here for benefits?"* These were just a few thoughts running through my mind. Sitting there, I was afraid of what they would say. Will they say no? Will there be a shooting? Watching the security officers with their guns and other gadgets attached to the belt on their waist, should have made me feel safe, but instead, I felt like I was in a warzone waiting room. I was there physically but not mentally.

As I think back about my experience with the Social Security office, I wonder how a person could explain that they cannot walk when their appearance gives a different message. There are times that I could not walk, but you could not see what was causing my disability because nothing was wrong with my legs.

Should we wear t-shirts that says, I am often so depressed that I cannot get out of bed? While I can occasionally get out of bed after a mental struggle, and leave the house without being afraid that something horrible will happen, there are some people who do not leave the house period.

What can we tell our loved ones so they are able to understand how to help us? I often wonder to myself, but because I don't understand it, it's hard to know what to tell others. It puzzles me on how many ways that our minds effect our body and how different depression may be for some people. Some stop eating while others may overeat. There were times I couldn't eat, but I did not need a gastrologist because there was nothing wrong with my digestive system. I needed to consult with a psychiatrist because I had mental issues.

Thinking about my panic attacks, some caused me to be nauseous while others just caused anxiety. I am here with hundreds of people looking for financial assistance for something that I cannot explain – an invisible disability.

SOCIAL SECURITY OFFICE VISIT

When they called my number, I walked down a long hall that had nothing but small glass windows, sectioned off with a partition and two chairs in each section. This office set-up reminded me of what I saw on TV when people visited their loved ones in prison.

"Are you Karen," the lady behind the glass window asked?

"Yes, I am," I replied while fumbling through my purse looking for a tissue because I began to cry!!

"Have a seat. How may I help you?"

I began to explain that someone suggested that I hand deliver my paperwork for expedited services. The packet of over eight forms was submitted six weeks prior; however, additional information was requested. I was two days away from my ten-day deadline for submitting the paperwork before they would close my case completely. I handed her a large white envelope filled with papers that I completed to apply for disability. She opened the envelope, stood up, and walked away from her desk. I could not see where she was going or what she was doing because gray cubicles were facing the windows. *"Just why am I here?"* I thought to myself as tears slid down my cheeks then on to my blouse.

The representative made a phone call to the person handling my case. I waited all this time to find out that I could have provided the information over the phone. But then, I went down another long hall with more windows, just like the stations on the other side of the wall. With these many nameplates and office spaces, why were there still so many people in the waiting room? Oh, that's right. It was just before Thanksgiving and some people were on vacation. I understand because I wanted a vacation from my situation. I call it a "situation" because, during that time, I was too ashamed to put a name to it - mental illness.

Sitting there, I was scared they would ask me questions that would trigger anxiety causing me to burst into tears. But the process was not as painful as I had expected. This Social Security office only collected the data and paperwork to send to the main office in Austin. *"You will receive a phone call if someone has any questions. Otherwise, wait to get something in the mail telling you what to do next,"* she said as she handed me a copy of the documents that I submitted. Now I had to wait an additional six to eight weeks for a response from the

Social Security Disability Office.

DISABILITY DENIAL

After going back and forth with the Social Security office for over eight months, I received a denial letter. The letter stated that I was not disabled. Great news! Well, it depends on who you ask. Based on a recent survey, people with a mental illness believe they would be treated differently if the employer was aware of his or her illness. This dilemma causes some people to face the chances of being denied a job and disability.

DISABILITY APPEAL

Several people informed me that Social Security would deny you first, regardless of your disability. So, I appealed the disability letter by completing another set of forms that asked the same questions that I answered on the first set. I guess they wanted to check to see if my symptoms changed for better or worse, if I started working, if my answers were the same, or maybe this was to delay the application process. Each time I completed the papers, I found myself crying because some of the questions triggered my pain. The questions forced me to reflect on things that I was going through, but was not ready to discuss.

Social Security denied the original request and appeal. The message looked like a form letter that said, *"NO."* There were a lot more words on this, but I searched for, *"we are pleased to announce"* or *"we regret to inform you."* The way I process information, one statement means *"Yes,"* and the other statement means *"No."*

So, I skipped down to the end for the portion that said, *"If you disagree with this statement, let us know, but get a lawyer."* Okay, it did not say it exactly like that, but that was the bottom-line.

IT'S THE LAW

One day I was resting on the couch watching one of my regular programs on television. During a commercial break, there was an advertisement for a disability lawyer. The number flashed across the screen. They asked all the right questions.

"Have you filed for Social Security? Was your Social Security denied for disability for mental health? Disability for mental health is one of the most common things to be denied and harder to prove. Call us, and we can help you."

So, I called the number, asked for help, and they asked me a series of questions. After answering those questions, they sent me a packet to complete and sign. Although they agreed to handle my case, I learned the process could take up to two years and they couldn't guarantee we would win.

Financial advisors teach us to have a savings equivalent to our monthly expenses for six months, not two years. *"Seven hundred thirty days is a long time to be unemployed without financial assistance."* I thought to myself. What does a person do if they do not have twenty-four months in savings?

The disability office indirectly suggests that you retain a lawyer. It appears to be common for people to seek legal counsel when applying for disability for mental health.

The amount of your Social Security disability benefits that an attorney would receive is twenty percent of your backpay, not to exceed six-thousand dollars. They are unable to receive any of your monthly payments. If you or a loved one is considering filing for disability, hiring an attorney may be worth it in the end. The attorney only collects pay if they win your case.

At first, I was skeptical about the entire process, but then again, I asked myself, *"What do I have to lose? I am not employed now and I had no idea if I would ever work again."* I was mentally exhausted. With everything else that was going on, I was thinking the worst, *"The attorneys are out to get as much money as they can because they wanted the max of six-thousand dollars."* At that time, I did not realize that the process was not the attorney's rules but the government's rules.

My thoughts were all over the place now because of how I had been treated in the past. I knew the training wheels were off and it was time to take a chance, but I felt a sense of uneasiness.

"Why should this be any different?" I did not have anything to prove it was only my insecurities. I do not have trust issues. I have people lying and mistreating me issues.

Hear ye, hear ye, the reason why some people are not working, is not because they are lazy and want to depend on the government. Perhaps they are not able to obtain employment because some of the current rules and guidelines are not as effective as society wants us to believe. So now what happens, they lose their job, their home, and possibly their mind, what's next? Sometimes the systems and people who are put in place to help people hurt them.

Now, what do I do? Remove all of my postings, delete my website, search for a new identity, and become a **Missing Person**. Should I look for a job that would only accept me if I hide my mental illness? This time, no one will know that I suffer from panic attacks and depression. Period! The cycle begins again. The stigma remains.

11

HIDDEN IN PLAIN SIGHT

The train was my new transportation of choice. I only flew on an airplane when I had to, but I was too afraid to fly most times. I used to drive, but I never had to drive alone, and it seemed like the trip to St. Louis had gotten longer or further away as I grew older.

Whenever I booked my reservations, I looked for a day that had enough seats available so that I could ride on the lower level of the train. If there were no lower level seats available on my preferred day, I selected the day before or after. I preferred the lower level for several reasons, but one of them was because there were fewer people and fewer distractions.

You see, my disability was not visible. I could walk, but I was enabled by my fear. Some people find me to be very personable, but often I prefer being one-on-one or in smaller groups.

ALL ABOARD!

One cold snowy winter, I booked a lower level seat like usual. The walk from the station to the platform was as long as the train trip, I thought to myself. There were several passengers on this half-mile journey with me from the station to the train tracks. The sound from our feet was out of sync like that of horses walking on concrete. We strutted to the rhythm of the click-clacking of the wheels of our luggage. As we walked down a long hall, up an escalator, then down an elevator, I recall how glad I was that I checked most of my luggage.

Once I arrived on the platform, standing in line with others next to the train, I could hear the conductor give others instructions. *"You go to the third car; you go here to the lower level; you go to the second car."* The instructions were given to navigate passengers to their seats. Your destination was used to determine your seat assignment. Also, included on the front of your ticket was personal assistance information. Passengers that were going to the same city would sit in the same car. However, if you had a lower level seat, your destination did not matter. Everyone with a lower level seat assignment sat in the same area.

Towering over me was this six-foot, seven-inch-tall gentleman wearing a navy-blue jacket with a blue hat. As he took my ticket he said hurriedly, *"You go to the third car to the left."*

Before walking off, I remembered that the third car was not lower level seating.

"I booked a lower level seat, why are you sending me to the third car?" I turned to him and said.

"Your seat was changed." He replied in a cold, dry tone.

"But I purchased my ticket months ago, what happened to my

reserved seat?" I said while trying not to cry.

"Your reservations have been changed. There are no extra lower level seats. So, go to the last car on the left!"

"There were seats available when I booked my trip months ago!"

"That is not my problem. My responsibility is to make sure that people get on the train; you need to take that up with corporate."

Before I could respond, he walked toward the platform, then jumped on the train while shouting,
"All Aboard!"

I hurriedly tried to walk to the third car, where he was standing, but there was a long line of passengers trying to get on the train.

He continued walking away until he was out of my sight.
"What? Did he just totally dismiss me?" I was so upset that

I wanted to change my travel date. But I couldn't because I had already checked my luggage.

This incident showed me several things. One thing I experienced was, if you do not have a visible disability, some people may be judgmental and cruel. By my appearance, it looks like I can walk just fine, but depression is debilitating. What about the person who is claustrophobic, afraid of heights, or other non-physical disabilities? Should a person be treated differently because of their disability?

I discovered that you might not be able to change a situation, but you can control how you respond and manage it. Therefore, I made up my mind not to ride on the train for fifteen hours upset. Because there was nothing, anyone could do to correct the problem immediately. The only option I had at this point was to ride it out and deal with customer service when I reached my destination. This attitude gave me peace and favor with the upper deck attendant. He allowed me to have a row to myself for the entire ride as his way of apologizing for the treatment that I received from the conductor.

The train boarded late that night, so it wasn't long before I fell asleep. I also went to sleep, hoping to make the trip pass by faster. When I woke, the sun was up. We were almost home. There were two young men quietly sitting across from me engaged with their electronic devices. I thought it would be good to strike up a conversation with them to help make the trip go faster. I asked the gentlemen closest to the end of the aisle, *"Where are we?"* Before he could answer, the conductor made an announcement stating if anyone wanted breakfast, they had ten minutes to get to the dining car.

The older gentlemen gathered his belongings, then wiggled his way between the seats into the aisle to get breakfast.

People have said that I talk a lot. So, before I continued the conversation, I said, *"I like to talk, so don't let me bother you. I will go back to sleep because I love to sleep even more."* He chuckled as he responded while leaning his head closer to me and said, *"You are fine ma'am. I love to listen."*

We discovered that we attended the same church and just had small talk until he reached his destination. I had an opportunity to share my story with him about my new venture. I expressed to him that I was promoting mental health awareness and that he was the second person who recently made me feel good about talking. The first person was my life coach. I told her that I struggled because people said that I talk a lot. She said, *"You are a storyteller."* My eyes welled up, and I have been writing and telling stories ever since that day.

Now I understand why it was time for me to sit in the upper deck. I know that God wanted me up and around people to be able to use me to tell my testimony about how I cope with panic attacks. That was the day that I realized it was more to it than just being afraid. It was also deeper than medical, hereditary, situational, or post-traumatic stress. It was spiritual! I realized that God wanted me to share my story with others. I also realized that I could handle sitting in the upper deck.

How many times have you stayed in a situation that was comfortable because you did not know that you could handle a change? You have been riding a bike with training wheels to help you with your balance for so long you feel comfortable and safe. One day you are riding the bike; you are maintaining your balance; then you realize the training wheels are no longer scraping the ground. Unconsciously, you discover that it's beyond time to remove the training wheels. You can remove any fears keeping you from change.

12

BREAKING NEWS

The news is getting out. Karen is no longer working. I do not know what prison is like, but I felt like I was just rescued from a prison of some sort. I had been in an antagonistic situation that drained me mentally, physically, spiritually, and emotionally. I felt that I had no choice but to escape.

People who knew my gifts, talents and abilities were willing to help me find employment. But first, I needed to take a break. For over thirty years, I had been getting up before 5:00 a.m. at least five days a week. Some mornings I drove on every major freeway to get to the office, in some of the worst traffic. After sitting in a car for almost an hour each day, I sat behind a desk for sometimes ten to twelve hours a day. After a productive day at work, it was common for me to jet off to my son's basketball game or my daughter's swim meet. I often arrived home with hardly enough time to snatch a quick nap before repeating the cycle the next day. Oh, the joys of single parenting. I often wonder, *"How did I make it through those days?"*

CORPORATE STIGMA

One day, I received a phone call from a former employer. This person offered to help me get a job. They went on to say, *"Karen, you can do anything, and you are good at everything that you do. You work hard, learn fast, and working with you has been a pleasure. Let me know if there is anything that I can do to help you."* They went on to ask me if I considered what I wanted to do and recommended resources for me to check. They also offered to assist me with my resumé. But it was the last statement that startled me, yet helped me to realize that I was about to embark on new territory.

"You will have to take down your website and posting about panic attacks and depression until you get a job."

The person did not mean any harm by the comment, nevertheless, the recommendation further confirmed the stigma associated with mental health. I worked for top executives for over thirty years, and it did not affect my work. You and others did not know. But now that you know, I should hide behind a mask until I land a job? The stigma is an example of why some people do not talk about their health. I understand the HIPAA (Health Insurance Portability and Accountability Act of 1996) laws and personal reasons that people do not talk about their health issues and concerns. But a person who has other illnesses can get a job if they post something about their illness. During my research, I did not find anything that indicated that mental illness was contagious. Yet, others may be affected by being in the presence of someone with certain mental illnesses. I hope we can agree that several recent events around the world reveals that mental illness affects all of us directly or indirectly.

I welcomed the assistance, but I also shared that I wanted to work for a company that did not discriminate. I am searching for the CEO, CFO, COO or President who understands that my panic attacks will not hurt my productivity. Also, I hoped that they would realize my value and worth as they too may have a mental illness or have a family member that has a mental illness.

Realizing that decisions comes with consequences, I said that I do not want to work for anyone who has a problem with my blog. I am expressing my personal experience with panic attacks to provide information and resources to others. In addition to being eager to help others, I no longer want to be a **Missing Person**.

LET'S GET INTO THE WEEDS

Now that I have your attention. Some people prefer nontraditional methods to help them with their panic attack disorders such as smoking marijuana. People use cannabis for a variety of reasons. We are going to talk about how it relates to panic attacks and depression. If I knew the ONE remedy to manage panic attacks, I would let you know. We must remember that everyone's situation is different, and what works for some may not work for others.

I am not implying that I would smoke weed as a remedy for panic attacks. What I am doing is working for me. Yet, I am suggesting that those of you that have suffered from a panic attack, (pro or con to smoking weed), you should understand the yearning for an antidote. Someone very close to me who experienced panic attacks once said, *"I would not wish a panic attack on my worst enemy."*

I was always taught and still believe in abiding by the Holy Bible as it commands us to comply with the laws of the land in Romans 13:1-3. Here are some questions for you. If a person who received a felony for possession of weed could prove that they were using it to manage a mental illness; should they be granted a second chance? If the person has a clean record and only consumes marijuana as medication, should they be allowed at least one exemption? Should the charges be removed from their record under the conditions that they agree to seek professional help and receive a traditional treatment? Is it possible that they were unable to adequately describe their symptoms? Perhaps they were too embarrassed to inquire about their experience because of the stigma? Would seeking help hurt their chances of retaining employment or getting a job? What about the possibility of rejection from friends and family? Perhaps the lack of communication about the topic makes it more difficult to access information so that a person would know what to do to get the help necessary? Non-traditional methods, such as smoking marijuana are the choice for some, but not all.

One may say, there are a lot of resources available. But you have to realize a person who has a mental illness may perceive things differently. What seems logical to others may not be our story. The stigma creates a barrier that prevents people who suffer from a mental illness from accessing some of the resources available. Coping mechanisms may be different for everyone depending on their symptoms and disorder. It is essential to remember that panic attack remedies are not a *"one size fits all."*

It is vital to remember for people who suffer from panic attacks or depression that someone understands them, and the sickness diminishes quickly.

"Let every soul be subject unto the higher powers. For there is no power but of God: the powers that be are ordained of God.

Whosoever therefore resisteth the power, resisteth the ordinance of God: and they that resist shall receive to themselves damnation.

For rulers are not a terror to good works, but to the evil. Wilt thou then not be afraid of the power? do that which is good and thou shalt have praise of the same." (Romans 13: 1-3)

SURVIVE AND SNITCH

Did you know that the color for mental illness is green and that October 10th is World Mental Health Awareness Day? I want the subject openly discussed so that people can get the help needed to live a better quality of life. I did not realize that May was Mental Health Awareness Month until I started openly talking about my struggles with panic attacks.

At best, society should educate us about how to manage relationships with people who have different types of mental illnesses. I once worked with someone who showed signs of narcissism and someone else who was bi-polar. Would you offer a diabetic something to eat that is extremely high in carbohydrates or sugar? Accordingly, what are the things we can do or not do to avoid triggering someone's mental illness? I hope that we all agree that mental illness affects us all in some form or another.

13

From Pain to Purpose

The events before, during, or after my panic attacks had at least two things in common; loss and separation. The loss could have been voluntary (selling a home) or involuntary (losing a loved one). Nonetheless, these elements led me to panic, depression, and fear. Simply put, fear of the unknown.

If death and sickness triggered my panic attack, how was I able to press forward and work to become a licensed insurance agent? To do this, I studied over seventy hours and took a two-hour exam that covered things like sickness and death. It seemed that this experience forced me to come full circle.

IDENTIFY YOUR VALUE AND WORTH

During this journey, I was able to identify my value and worth. This encouraged me to set boundaries and expectations. Having boundaries helps me have less worry and less stress. Set boundaries and start living again!

These two things were vital to my recovery and helped me to manage my panic attacks. I had to change my perspective; set limits and have more reasonable expectations. For example, now that I know that what I hear and see affects me mentally, I choose to avoid obvious triggers. Furthermore, I choose not to watch the news daily or do things that would cause me to have an adverse emotional reaction or response.

If I inadvertently hear something that could cause me to panic or worry, I think to myself *"Lord, you knew that I would be in this place and at this time so if something happens to me, God ordained it."* Sometimes I recited silently, *"That is not my story."* Talking to myself and reassuring myself were things I did to prevent a downhill rabbit trail that would convince me I was going to face the unthinkable. One may say that I *"changed the station in my head."* A firm conscious choice was made to help me decide what I would see, hear or imagine. I also took control and decided on my responses to the thoughts, voices, and sights. It is up to me to determine if and how I am going to respond.

STAND FOR SOMETHING

I worked in the professional executive offices of corporate America for years, and I had become accustomed to handling my life the same way. I answered every phone call promptly, or I returned every phone call within twenty-four hours. But then I came to a realization; I get to set the rules for my life. It's my choice to answer every call, respond to every text immediately, and please the customer. This was not required nor a healthy habit for my personal life.

I realized that a lot of my expectations from working in corporate spilled over to my practices in personal life. I expected people to take my phone call, respond to my text, follow-up, and communicate. The sooner you realize that you cannot hire and fire people like they are co-workers and employees, the better. Not only do I choose when and whom to call and accept calls from, but I also turn off my cell phone completely. Yes, you too, can do it!

When I was a teenager, my mother purchased a poster as a souvenir for me from her trip to a church convention. To my surprise, it was not a Bible verse. It included a quote attributed to Alexander Hamilton that read: *"Stand for something, or you will fall for anything!"* I have not been able to find that poster physically, but I am thankful to God that I was able to locate it again mentally. Standing for something has given me purpose and the ability to manage my stress levels while turning my pain into motivation and strength.

14

LEFT A NOTE

People often asked me if I knew what caused my panic attacks? For years, the answer was No! Over the past few years, the panic attacks increased. The frequency of the attacks allowed me to become more aware of some triggers and ways to avoid them. But I am still not always sure of the cause.

Journaling my panic attacks and tracing them back to things that happened leading up to the attack helps me tremendously. I use this information as a reminder as to how I survived, then I write positive affirmations to repeat during an episode.

Jotting down my thoughts encouraged me immensely. Try journaling your daily experiences. Sometimes I wrote whatever I was thinking or feeling that day. I may never read it, but it felt good to get things off my mind. In case you have similar experiences, I want you to know that you are not alone. Knowing that others experienced the same things and survived gives me hope. I pray that it encourages you too! Here are a few of the notes that I wrote in my journal to clear my head.

MY JOURNAL – BEDSIDE BAPTIST

Bedside Baptist - Here it is another Sunday and what am I doing? I am in bed; however, I want to attend church, but for some reason, I just cannot get out of bed.

I'm done! I am going to find a doctor and go see them first thing tomorrow. Why tomorrow, I cannot get up today. I think I will stay in my room for the rest of the week and just write.

Why some people plummet into depression is becoming more evident every day. I don't want to feel like this, but it is becoming my norm. It is weird because it is a safe place where I can hide. That's it! A hiding place! Depression is a temporary secluded place to escape the troubles of the world. Not a world crisis, my crisis. Stuff that I cannot change. I search deep within to discover what is bothering me. Why is it that the things that made me the happiest, do not make me happy anymore?

I have discovered that no matter what you have or do not have, your peace and happiness come from within not from what you possess. I thought being alone was why I was depressed, but that is not it. I feel alone even though I am surrounded by other people. I feel more alone now than I did when I was actually by myself. At least when I am by myself, I understand, or should I say I can justify being alone.

MY JOURNAL – CHURCH HURT

Another Sunday just here alone. As a Christian, the first place you would think I would run to for help is the church. Having experienced so much hurt because of politics and religious activities, I find it difficult at times to enjoy going to church. The place where I was once going to for healing is now the source of my pain.

God has given me the peace needed, so I can attend any church without being haunted by the pains of my past. I am sure others like me find themselves lost and confused because they used to receive healing at church. This subject is also a book by itself. *Church Hurt – Touch Your Neighbor* ©

MY JOURNAL – NOTE TO SELF

For those of you that choose to "judge" people with a mental illness, thanks! Your biased view is one of the reasons I am speaking out!

MY JOURNAL – TAKE YOUR MEDICINE

Today is May 2019, and I realized that medicine is still necessary. I keep telling people to take their medicine, but I stopped taking my medicine only to see if I am better or if I am just better because of the medication. Day three and I can tell the difference. Little things aggravate me. I am feeling depressed. I also feel lightheaded when I think about specific experiences, people who did things to me in my past and fear of failure.

Here I go again, about to cry. I feel lonely, even though I am not alone. I feel helpless, although I am full of knowledge. I don't trust anyone. I don't want to talk to anyone. My doctor recommended that I consult with him before making any changes in taking my medication. He told me that if I wanted to stop, he would provide a process and plan for me to stop taking the medication, and this was not something that I should do suddenly. Most of the times when I stopped taking my medicine, it was purely accidental. I forgot about it because I was feeling so much better.

If your medication is working, you (should) feel better. There are several reasons a person may stop taking their medication. For instance, the pill may cause you to gain weight, sleep more, or some other adverse side effect. It took three to four days before I felt the impact of discontinuing the medication. This experience showed me several things. If you stop taking it suddenly, you may have an adverse reaction. Different types of medications work for different people. Work with your physician to see what is best for you. Do not give up. Some people may not have to take medication for extended periods, but your doctor will tell you how to wean yourself off the prescription gradually.

15

ANONYMOUS TIP LINE

Some people have panic attacks frequently, while others may only have one or two in a lifetime. My panic attacks developed in many ways, but the symptoms peaked within minutes.

There are many ways to answer the question, *"What is a panic attack?"* This article from Mayo Clinic's website describes it best for me.

"A panic attack is a sudden episode of intense fear that triggers severe physical reactions when there is no real danger or apparent cause. Panic attacks can be very frightening. When panic attacks occur, you might think you're losing control, having a heart attack or even dying."

I Am Not A Licensed Professional - Therefore, I strongly urge you to seek advice from a physician or licensed professional before attempting any of the methods mentioned in my book. I am sharing my personal story to let you view the mind of a person who suffers from panic attacks and depression.

Seek Professional Help - Call 911 if you have a life-threatening emergency. Do not be your own physician. If you choose to be your own doctor, it's important to seek a second opinion from another medical professional to confirm what you may already know.

Journal Your Experience Daily, Good and Bad - Journaling provided me with an outlet to get things off my mind. It showed me what was similar and gave me hope for a positive outcome. It also helped me to identify my triggers. I used my notes as a reference to learn what worked and what did not.

Drinking Cold Water - There were times that I was able to ease the symptoms of a panic attack by drinking cold water. It soothed the nerves in my stomach and prevented my panic attack from escalating.

What You See and Hear Matters - I noticed that watching certain things on television or listening to certain things on the radio, had an adverse influence on me. Therefore, I am very selective about the TV shows I watch. Comedy and Family Dramas are safe for me. I recall my son playfully saying, *"Mom, you watch the same television shows and movies as an eight-year-old!"* I giggled, *"If that is what it takes to avoid an attack, I am okay with that."* Set boundaries for yourself.

Ask Questions - If you encounter a person experiencing a panic attack in your presence, first ask them if they think they are having an attack or need to go to the hospital? The symptoms are very similar to a heart attack. Don't ask questions or say things like, *"are you having a heart attack?"* That statement alone could cause a person's panic attack to escalate. They may not have the presence of mind to make the proper decision. You may be able to rule out a heart attack by asking specific questions but each person is different. It is always best to seek professional help. While waiting on professional help, calmly ask questions that show you care and support their decision to go to the hospital or not. I was often too embarrassed to go to the ER but equally afraid not to get professional help.

Stay Calm - Staying calm may help keep that person relaxed. Calmly assure them that they will be okay. If you appear nervous, that may make them more anxious. Sometimes the way a person looked at me made me think they noticed something horribly wrong, so I panicked even more. While helping a person that is having a panic attack, try to watch what you say and your facial expressions whenever possible.

Breathe - Ask them to inhale and exhale taking slow deep breaths. I usually have to close my eyes when doing this. Focusing on breathing correctly may help take your mind off the attack.

Get Out of the House - A person who suffers from panic attacks may stay home more often and avoid social gatherings because they are concerned that they will have a panic attack in public. It's okay to stay home sometimes, but try to get out and explore new things. Take a walk or exercise. Vitamin D from the sun is helpful to some.

Take A Break - With modern technology dominating our lifestyles, we are basically forced to sleep less. Televisions are on all night, cell phones are constantly dinging, and electronic devices are brightening the room and possibly interrupting our sleep.

Get Some Rest! And Sleep - Sleep and rest are two different things because I rest while watching television. I sleep while snoring. I notice that I can be a little more agitated if I have not rested well. Avoid people and situations that may cause you to act differently because of your lack of sleep.

What a person thinks about you is none of your business. This statement was used to advise me not to worry about what others may say about me. Of course, this is difficult to do. It's important to know and believe what God says about you and who you are. One spring, while visiting my mom, she sang her version of the song by Dorothy Love Coats, *"That's Enough,"* sometimes two and three times a day. I felt as if my mom used the song to help me by giving me something to use to fight the spiritual warfare I was experiencing in my life. She did not know how I felt because we hadn't discussed anything. However, she could feel it as a mother.

"There is always somebody talking about me, but really I don't mind. They try to stop and block my progress, most of the time. The mean things they say can't make me feel bad, because I got a friend that they never had. I got Jesus, and that's enough."

I sang this song to give me courage every time I thought that someone was talking about me. Find your song. What God says about you is what truly matters.

Identify Your Purpose - Study your Bible. Write positive quotes down and recite them as often as possible. Placing positive affirmations on your mirrors, in your car, or wherever you spend most of your time may be helpful.

Support System - Surround yourself with positive people who believe in you and will keep you encouraged. The church is a great place to attend for worship and to learn about God's plan for your life and your purpose. However, some churches do not have the resources to help with mental health from a medical standpoint. From a spiritual perspective, support from your church is key. I found myself upset when I did not get the help that I needed from the church to cope with my depression and panic attacks. People said things like, *"You worry too much!"* Others ignored my cry for help altogether. But there are some churches that God has designed specifically to minister to hurting people, and others may have the resources for you to get the help needed.

Awareness – Talking about panic attacks and mental health with your family and friends can make a difference. I am beginning to understand why some family members did not want to talk about mental health. Discussing your mental illness may uncover their struggles. They may also be ashamed for others to know about your mental illness. Since I have been blogging and openly talking about mental health, I have been doing much better. I still had a few panic attacks, a couple more severe than others, but it helps to know that my friends and loved ones know what to do to help me.

Acceptance - Mental illness is not something that you can *"just get over"* or *"let go."* Studies show mental illnesses may be hereditary. Talk to your family. Maybe others can share ways to help you cope with your illness. It may be something that you will have to live with but knowing how to manage it will make a lasting difference.

Action - Even if you do not want to talk about it openly to others, I encourage you to seek professional help.

16

FOUND

There are several types of mental illnesses. Panic attacks and depression are what I experienced. I prefer not to discuss the others because I am not confident that I could give them justice like a person who has the disorder.

Nevertheless, my ultimate goal is to eliminate the stigma associated with ALL MENTAL ILLNESSES.

Each day has not been easy. Honestly, I do not encourage everyone to speak out about their mental issues. Others may look at you differently. Some good and not so good may come of it. For instance, speaking publicly may prevent you from certain job opportunities. I know that the law states that employers are not supposed to discriminate due to disabilities, blah, blah blah, but they do. So, if you are not economically prepared to accept the possibility of rejection from some employers, do not speak publicly. Nevertheless, don't let people discourage you from seeking professional help. In the least, talk to a person you trust. Overall, approximately ninety percent of the people I surveyed were encouraging and supportive. Just be prepared for either response; positive or negative.

Be careful that people do not take advantage of your vulnerability. Sometimes others benefit from your illness. Consequently, don't be surprised if they treat you differently as you improve. My illness gave some people the power to control me. Now that I have strength, they no longer choose to associate with me. While this is hurtful, it is still not as painful as having a panic attack.

To make a point in my story, I deliberately tried to avoid using the word "anxiety" because many people have or may experience anxiety or anxiousness. Some people encounter anxiety once or twice and may never have to face it again. I firmly believe that there is a noticeable difference between a person who has panic attacks and someone who experiences anxiousness. I must clarify this misconception because I have struggled with both. For me, there is a noticeable distinction. There is also a difference between someone who has one panic attack, and people who have panic disorder.

| Anxiety vs Panic Attack
Disclaimer: I am not a licensed professional. This description is based on my personal experience and research. ||
Anxiousness	Panic Attack
Your heart starts to beat rapidly.	Your heart **suddenly** starts to beat rapidly.
You start hyperventilating.	You start hyperventilating.
You may start to sweat.	You may start to sweat.
You know why you are anxious (i.e. you are the speaker at a public event, job interview, or you are about to take an important exam, etc.)	You **may or may not know** the reason for the sudden rapid heartbeat
Emotion: You may have a fear of failure, humiliation, or rejection, etc.	Emotion: You feel like you are about to die or face the unthinkable.

A missing person in common terms is a person whose fate or whereabouts are unknown. When God told me to title my book, **Missing Person**, I had no idea why. There were times I felt that I was wandering through life alone because I did not believe anyone understood me. But I never thought I was "missing." Today, it makes sense.

In the Book of Genesis, God asks Adam, *"Where are you?"* Did God lose Adam? When Adam responded, *"I heard thy voice in the garden, and I was afraid, because I was naked; and I hid myself."* God asked, *"Who told you that?"*

Some of us depend on others for validation. Often comparing ourselves to others in efforts to measure our value and worth. Don't let what you "think" people would say keep you from getting help, nor should you let it dictate how you feel about yourself. I finally realized that my shame and my concerns about the opinion of others forced me into hiding. Perhaps like God wanted Adam to think about his fate and whereabouts, we should do the same. Why are you hiding? Who told you that you were crazy? Where are you? Are you missing? Who told you that you were missing? God wants us to seek Him for answers to life's most difficult questions.

Some people get up in the morning and go about the day with little or no effort. While others struggle to get out of bed, not to mention the house. This scenario is why I believe that people who have to make it through the day while managing a mental illness are NOT CRAZY; we are COURAGEOUS!

Now that I know who I am, I am no longer ashamed. It took this twelve-month journey to discover the reason I was a **Missing Person** was because I had low self-esteem. God did not lose me! I did not realize there were so many others who were missing too. While some may not admit it now, I am hopeful they will someday, and if nothing else obtain the help needed. Though people may leave you, God will never leave you nor forsake you. He knows where you are. So it's time for you to come out of hiding.

I am grateful and delighted to report that Karen Metcalfe has been **FOUND**.

And the LORD *God called unto Adam, and said unto him, Where art thou?*

And he said, I heard thy voice in the garden, and I was afraid, because I was naked; and I hid myself. (Genesis 3:9-10)

A NEW SONG

The old song, *"Don't Nobody Like Me"* was written by someone whom I love tremendously. My baby brother was predestined to be a songwriter and singer.

I have a new song to sing.

"Beautiful Day"
By Tony Metcalfe

Hear me when I call, O God of my righteousness: thou hast enlarged me when I was in distress; have mercy upon me and hear my prayer.

O ye sons of men, how long will ye turn my glory into shame? How long will ye love vanity, and seek after leasing? Selah.

But know that the Lord hath set apart him that is godly for himself: the Lord will hear when I call unto him.

Stand in awe, and sin not: commune with your own heart upon your bed, and be still. Selah.

Offer the sacrifices of righteousness and put your trust in the Lord.

Many say, Who will shew us any good? Lord, lift thou the light of thy countenance upon us.

Thou hast put gladness in my heart, more than in the time that their corn and their wine increased.

I will both lay me down in peace, and sleep: for thou, Lord, only makest me dwell in safety.

ABOUT THE AUTHOR

Karen Annette Metcalfe spent over thirty years working in the executive offices for the banking industry, a non-profit organization, and hospital industry. She studied business administration and accounting in Missouri. She is the tenth child of thirteen children and the mother of two adult children. Karen is the President and CEO of Karen's Key Concepts, LLC. Karen currently lives in Texas.

***

Born in Missouri, I grew up when playing outside until the illumination of the street light signified curfew. During these days, racing in the middle of the street barefoot, playing jacks on the front porch, jumping to a game of hopscotch on the sidewalks, and hitting or kicking a ball in empty parking lots were the norm.

I was raised in a Pentecostal church and attended church three to four days a week. Growing up with a large family, I never recall arriving home to an empty house or missing a meal.

As a teenager, I spent numerous hours playing basketball for a girls' team or a pickup game with the guys. When I was not playing basketball, I was watching the boys' games, keeping the scorebook, or working the scoreboard.

As I became old enough to drive, I was at work or a skating rink rolling to the smooth jazz sounds of Al Jarreau and the rhythm of Bell Biv Devo.

I volunteered for many churches, schools and community events, including coaching a girls' basketball team.

After years of suffering from depression and panic attacks, I finally have the courage to share my story. I am determined to bring awareness to empower others who are perhaps ashamed to get help and eliminate the stigma about mental illness.

While I was writing this book, I suffered from depression and had a few panic attacks. But writing and speaking willingly about my experiences have undoubtedly transformed my life. I may have depression, but depression no longer has me.

Through prayer, medicine, and shamelessly discussing my struggles, I no longer suffer in silence. Throughout my journey, I have uncovered various resources and individuals who can offer assistance with managing or overcoming challenges that some people with a mental illness encounter.

I am thankful to God that I am no longer a **MISSING PERSON** and for giving me the strength and courage to let others know that they are not alone!